AN   2010

THE CIVIL WAR

VOLUME 6

= Lincoln Abraham - Mobile Bay, Battle of =

GROLIER

Published 2004 by Grolier, an imprint of Scholastic Library Publishing
Sherman Turnpike
Danbury, Connecticut 06816

Set ISBN: 0-7172-5883-1
Volume ISBN: 0-7172-5889-0

Library of Congress Cataloging-in-Publication Data
The Civil War
         p.cm.
    Includes bibliographical references (p.) and index.
    Contents: v. 1. Abolition–Camp followers—v. 2. Camp life–Custer, George A.—v. 3. Daily Life–Flags—v. 4.Florida–Hill, Ambrose P.—v. 5. Home front, Confederate–Legacy of the Civil War—v. 6. Lincoln, Abraham–Mobile Bay, Battle of—v. 7. Money and Banking–Politics, Confederate—v. 8. Politics, Union–Shenandoah Valley—v. 9. Sheridan, Philip H.–Trade—v. 10. Training–Zouaves.

    ISBN 0-7172-5883-1 (set: alk paper)—ISBN 0-7172-5884-X (v.1: alk paper)—
ISBN 0-7172-5885-8 (v.2: alk paper)—ISBN 0-7172-5886-6 (v.3: alk paper)—
ISBN 0-7172-5887-4 (v.4: alk paper)—ISBN 0-7172-5888-2 (v.5: alk paper)—
ISBN 0-7172-5889-0 (v.6: alk paper)—ISBN 0-7172-5890-4 (v.7: alk paper)—
ISBN 0-7172-5891-2 (v.8: alk paper)—ISBN 0-7172-5892-0 (v.9: alk paper)—
ISBN 0-7172-5893-9 (v.10: alk paper)

    1. United States—History—Civil War, 1861–1865—Encyclopedias, Juvenile. [United States—History—Civil War, 1861–1865—Encyclopedias.] 1. Grolier (Firm)

    E468.C613 2004
    973.7'03—dc22

    2003049315

For information address the publisher:
Grolier
Sherman Turnpike,
Danbury, Connecticut 06816

FOR THE BROWN REFERENCE GROUP PLC
Project Editor: Emily Hill
Deputy Editor: Jane Scarsbrook
Designer: Paul Griffin
Picture Researcher: Becky Cox

Maps: David Atkinson
Indexer: Kay Ollerenshaw
Managing Editor: Tim Cooke
Consultants: Professor James I. Robertson Jr,
                          Virginia Technical Institute and
                          State University
                          Dr. Harriet E. Amos Doss,
                          University of Alabama in Birmingham

Printed and bound in Singapore

ABOUT THIS BOOK

The Civil War was one of the turning points in U.S. history. The bitter "War between Brothers" cast a shadow that reaches to the present day. For the North the war began in determination to preserve the Union and ended as a crusade to free the slaves. For the South the conflict was the inevitable result of tensions between state and federal power that some argue remain unresolved. In its cavalry charges and sieges the war echoed wars of previous centuries; in its rifled weapons and its huge casualty figures—an estimated 620,000 soldiers died in four years of fighting—it looked forward to the world wars of the 20th century. This set of 10 books tells the stories of the key events, individuals, and battles of the struggle that split the nation. The alphabetically arranged entries also cover the social and political context of the fighting, and describe the involvement of every state in the war.

The Civil War was the first widely photographed war, and most of the images in the set were taken during the conflict itself. Most of the illustrations are also from contemporary sources, including the "special artists" who were sent to depict the battle action by newspaper editors. There are also numerous boxes giving eyewitness descriptions of individuals' experiences in battle or on the home front. Each entry ends with a list of cross-references to entries on related subjects elsewhere in the set. They will enable you to follow the subjects you are interested in and build your knowledge. At the end of each book there is a useful further reading list that includes websites, a glossary of special terms, and an index covering all 10 volumes.

Text: Harriet Amos Doss, Charles Bowery, Cynthia
          Brandimarte, Tom Brown, Jacqueline Campbell,
          Gregg Cantrell, Chris Capozzola, Janet Coryell, Anita
          Dalal, Alan C. Downs, Larry Gara, Mark Grimsley,
          Anthony Hall, Tim Harris, Herman Hattaway, Edward
          Horton, R. Douglas Hurt, Ted Karamanski, Phil
          Katcher, Rachel Martin, Robert Myers, Henry
          Russell, John David Smith, Karen Utz, Chris Wiegand

Contents

Lincoln, Abraham

The Civil War threatened the survival of the Union like no other event in the history of the United States. The crisis called for an exceptional leader, and the nation found that leader in the 16th president, Abraham Lincoln (1809–1865).

Lincoln was an unlikely choice for president. He was born in a one-room log cabin in Hardin County, Kentucky, on February 12, 1809, the son of Nancy Hanks and Thomas Lincoln. His father was a poor frontier farmer and could provide his son with little formal education. Lincoln later said he went to school "by littles"—in all for less than a year. Lincoln's mother died when he was nine, and the family moved twice before Lincoln was 22, first to Indiana and then to Illinois. As a young man in Illinois Lincoln held

Abraham Lincoln, photographed by Mathew Brady in 1864. William Herndon, Lincoln's law partner, described him as often looking "woe-struck."

a number of jobs, including keeping store in New Salem and splitting rails for fences. He also served briefly in the Illinois militia in 1832. Despite his lack of schooling, Lincoln educated himself to a high level with borrowed books and participated in a local debating society.

In 1834 Lincoln was elected to the Illinois legislature as a member of the Whig Party. He went on to serve four terms, and during these years he studied law and settled in the new state capital, Springfield. By the 1840s he was a successful lawyer. In 1842 he married Mary Todd, a young woman from a wealthy Kentucky banking family. Four years later he was elected to the House of Representatives. As a congressman he opposed the United States' war with Mexico (1846–1848). This was an unpopular stance, and he was not reelected. Lincoln returned to his law practice in Springfield but remained active in Whig politics.

Republican candidate

The Kansas–Nebraska Act of 1854, which potentially opened up the Northern territories to slavery, outraged Lincoln. He joined the new Republican Party, which was opposed to the westward expansion of slavery, and in 1858 the party nominated him for the Senate. Lincoln's performance in seven public debates against his Democratic opponent in Illinois, Stephen A.

Douglas, brought him to national prominence. During this campaign Lincoln made a statement that emphasized the crisis the nation was facing: "A house divided against itself cannot stand. I believe this government cannot endure permanently half slave and half free."

When the Republican national convention met in May 1860, Lincoln was one of several candidates for the presidential nomination. His principal opponent, Senator William H. Seward of New York, was thought too radical in his antislavery views, so Lincoln won the nomination. In the November election he received 39.8 percent of the popular vote and won the election with 180 of the 303 electoral votes.

Taking the nation to war
In the slaveholding states not one electoral vote was cast for Lincoln. By the time he took office in March 1861, seven slaveholding states had seceded from the Union. Lincoln did not want to respond aggressively and push the remaining eight slave states to secede. However, when the Confederacy demanded that Union troops surrender forts in Confederate states, Lincoln refused to give them up. Here he acted against the advice of his cabinet. In April Confederate forces attacked Fort Sumter, South Carolina. Congress was not in session, but Lincoln acted swiftly, issuing a call for 75,000 volunteers to join the Union army and suspending habeas corpus (the right not to be imprisoned without trial). Until July 4, when Congress met, Lincoln effectively conducted the war alone. Accusations of dictatorship, which continued throughout his presidency, were first made in these early months.

Commander-in-chief
Lincoln was equally decisive as commander-in-chief of the Union forces. At the start of the war General Winfield Scott submitted a war strategy known as the "Anaconda Plan," which advised defeating the Confederacy by means of a blockade. Lincoln accepted some parts of Scott's plan, but he also insisted on invading the South at multiple points. This action set a pattern for Lincoln as commander-in-chief: He listened to his generals but made his own decisions.

Some historians believe that Lincoln's lack of formal military training may have been an advantage. Most Civil War generals had been trained in

An illustrated print of Lincoln's Emancipation Proclamation. With this executive order, which came into effect on January 1, 1863, Lincoln freed more than 3 million slaves in the Confederate states.

the strategies of the Napoleonic Wars (1792–1815), but the size of Civil War armies and the deadliness of modern weapons called for new ways of thinking about warfare. Lincoln was not blinkered by formal training. Instead, he was able to apply his intelligence and devise strategies that often contradicted the military textbooks. During the course of the war Lincoln became one of the most able commanders-in-chief that the nation has ever had.

Lincoln's ideas about how the war should be fought brought him into conflict with many of his generals. Early in the war he placed George B. McClellan in command of the Army of the Potomac, with orders to invade northern Virginia and capture the Confederate capital, Richmond. Lincoln removed McClellan from command following his failure to pursue the retreating Confederates after the Battle of Antietam (Sharpsburg) in September 1862. It was a bold move, since McClellan was popular with his men and the Northern public alike. Lincoln subsequently fired several more generals who failed to carry out his ideas. In each case Lincoln displayed strong executive leadership.

Chief executive

As president Lincoln was also chief executive officer of the U. S. government. Unlike Confederate President Jefferson Davis, Lincoln resisted the temptation to become involved in too much detail. Instead, he chose able men to head the major departments of the government, and then he generally left them alone. This approach carried risks, because incompetent or dishonest officials could cause a great deal of trouble, but Lincoln largely avoided such problems because he was a good judge of character (see box opposite).

Party leader

Lincoln also had responsibilities as the leader of his political party. The Republican Party was barely five years old when he took office. It was composed of former Whigs and Democrats, and its members had a wide range of opinions on key issues such as slavery. Lincoln worked hard to keep the Republican coalition together throughout the war. He knew that he needed the support of Congress and the public to win the war and to be reelected for a second term in 1864. To achieve this broad support, he included former Whigs and former Democrats in his cabinet and appointed men of all political backgrounds to commands in the Union military.

Lincoln walked a tightrope on the slavery question, knowing that if he moved too strongly against slavery, he would alienate conservatives. At the same time, he faced pressure from abolitionists, who wanted him to declare all slaves free immediately. Unpopular issues such as the military draft and the arrest of political opponents posed political risks, but Lincoln always justified his decisions with eloquence and feeling. For example, when he was criticized for

A color print based on a photograph by Mathew Brady showing Abraham Lincoln reading to his youngest son, Thomas. Lincoln nicknamed him "tadpole," which was shortened to "Tad."

banishing peace agitator Clement L. Vallandigham without trial in spring 1863, Lincoln asked, "Must I shoot a simple-minded soldier boy who deserts while I must not touch a hair of a wily agitator who induces him to desert?" Finally, he was careful not to ignore nonmilitary Republican programs such as the Homestead Act of 1862.

One of Lincoln's greatest and most important assets was the way he interpreted his power. His critics often charged that he trampled on the Constitution. Lincoln's answer was that he was not afraid to sacrifice one-tenth of the Constitution to save the other nine-tenths. He was daring and innovative in his use of presidential power, making extensive use of executive orders. The greatest of these was the Emancipation Proclamation, which came into effect on January 1,

LINCOLN'S APPOINTEES

Lincoln made some excellent appointments. For example, he selected William H. Seward for the important post of secretary of state. Seward initially believed Lincoln to be unintelligent and unfit for the presidency, but Lincoln overlooked this personal slight. Seward became Lincoln's most trusted adviser and did an outstanding job as secretary of state. Lincoln made a similarly objective choice for treasury secretary. Salmon P. Chase of Ohio disliked the president, but Lincoln knew that Chase had a good financial mind and was well connected in the banking world. Chase never got over his resentment of Lincoln, but he performed well. He resigned late in 1864, and Lincoln then appointed him chief justice. Lincoln also showed faith in Ulysses S. Grant, who began the war in obscurity, handicapped by a reputation as a drunkard. Lincoln noted that even when Grant failed, he made no excuses and kept fighting. The president rewarded Grant's persistence with increasingly important assignments. After Grant's victory at Chattanooga, Tennessee, in November 1863 Lincoln promoted him to general-in-chief of all Union armies. Together they devised campaigns that finally won the war.

A painting by F. B. Carpenter depicting Lincoln reading the Emancipation Proclamation to the cabinet in July 1862. Seward is seated in profile on the right, and Chase stands on the left.

An engraving showing Lincoln's second inauguration on March 4, 1865. Chief Justice Salmon P. Chase administers the oath of office.

1863. Lincoln accepted that slavery could only be abolished by state-level action or by an amendment to the Constitution—neither of which were politically possible at that time. When he decided to strike a blow against slavery, he therefore did it by issuing a presidential proclamation. He justified the measure on the grounds of "military necessity," which is why it was limited to states in rebellion rather than applying to the whole country. For this reason the proclamation did not free slaves in Union territory.

The war's end

Lincoln's leadership held the Union cause together through the difficult first three years of the war. By mid-1864, with the fall of Atlanta, the tide had clearly turned in favor of the North. He won the November 1864 election against Democrat George B. McClellan by 212 electoral votes to 21. On April 9, 1865, Lincoln received the news of

Confederate General Robert E. Lee's surrender at Appomattox. A month earlier he had outlined his broad philosophy for the postwar reconstruction of the seceded states in his second inaugural address, stating that the Union should be reconstructed "with malice toward none, and charity for all." The difficult task of putting the nation back together was left for others, however, because on April 14 Lincoln was assassinated by John Wilkes Booth during a theater performance in Washington. He died the next day.

With the possible exception of George Washington, no other American leaders have had such an impact on the survival and development of the nation. Lincoln's emancipation of the slaves and his eloquent speeches also gave meaning to the Civil War for future generations. With his actions and words Lincoln reshaped American democracy and gave the nation "a new birth of freedom."

Lincoln's assassination

Shortly after the end of the war President Lincoln was assassinated as he sat watching a play with his wife. Following the assassination, a wave of grief swept the North, while in the South many feared Northern reprisals.

On the evening of April 14, 1865, President Lincoln and his wife, Mary Todd Lincoln, were spending a pleasant time at Ford's Theatre in Washington, D.C. They were watching a performance of a very popular British comedy of the day, *Our American Cousin,* in the company of Lincoln's military aide, Major Henry Rathbone, and Rathbone's fiancée, Clara Harris. The president's bodyguard had slipped out for a drink.

The shooting

Shortly after 10:00 P.M. the actor John Wilkes Booth entered the theater, where he was well known, and made his way unopposed to the presidential box. Timing his entry to coincide with a line from the play that Booth knew would draw a big laugh, he opened the door to the box, stepped in, and shot the president in the back of the head.

Major Rathbone tried to grapple with Booth, forcing him to the railing of the box. Booth then leaped over, caught the spur of his boot on the flag draped over the railing, and crashed to the stage below. He suffered a broken leg in the fall but immediately clambered to his feet. Shouting "*Sic semper tyrannis*! [So it always is with tyrants] The South is avenged!" he fled the theater and made his getaway on a waiting horse.

Meanwhile, a doctor in the audience rushed to the box to find the president

A printed broadside issued five days after Lincoln's death offering a reward for the capture of his murderer. A portion of the reward money was shared among the 26 soldiers who cornered John Wilkes Booth in a tobacco barn.

slumped forward unconscious, the bullet having lodged just behind his right eye. Although Lincoln was still breathing, it was clear that he had suffered a mortal wound. He was carried to a boarding house across the road where, despite the best efforts of doctors, he died a little before 7:30 A.M. the following day.

CONSPIRACY THEORIES

After the assassination Lincoln's widow and some members of Congress were convinced that Vice President Andrew Johnson had a hand in the crime. Mary Todd Lincoln wrote to a friend in March 1866: "that miserable inebriate Johnson had cognizance of my husband's death." Todd Lincoln's suspicion rested on a calling note that Booth left for Johnson's private secretary on the day of the assassination. Beyond this evidence suggesting that Johnson was acquainted with Booth, the theory had no basis in fact. A book was published in the 1930s that made a case for the involvement of Secretary of War Edwin M. Stanton. It portrayed Stanton's behavior around the time of the assassination as suspicious, suggesting that he deliberately refused to release from duty a bodyguard that Lincoln had requested for the evening. More recent examinations have completely discredited the theory that Stanton was a shadowy figure behind Booth's plot.

A third theory, which again lacks supporting evidence, argues that a plot to kidnap Lincoln and later to murder him was hatched at the highest levels of the Confederate government, and that Booth was a Confederate agent who organized the deed. According to this theory, the Confederate government believed that Lincoln had sanctioned the killing of Jefferson Davis in the course of a raid on Richmond and therefore considered Lincoln a legitimate war target.

Meanwhile, Booth had escaped Washington, but on April 26 he was surrounded by soldiers and trapped in a tobacco barn near Bowling Green in Virginia. When he refused to surrender, the barn was set alight. Booth became silhouetted through the flames, and one of the soldiers shot him in the neck. He was dragged from the burning building still alive but died later that day.

The conspirators

While no one disputes that Booth was the assassin, it is also certain that he was acting with coconspirators. At the same time as Lincoln's assassination Lewis Payne forced his way into the home of William H. Seward, Lincoln's secretary of state. Payne tried to slit Seward's throat as he lay in his bed recovering from an accident. Seward was saved by the surgical collar he was wearing. Booth also instructed George Atzerodt to kill Vice President Andrew Johnson. However, Atzerodt did not attempt to carry out his assignment. Within days Payne and Atzerodt were arrested, as were David Herold, Samuel Arnold, Michael O'Laughlen, and Mary Surratt, whose boarding house had served as the meeting place for the conspirators. Payne, Herold, Atzerodt, and Surratt were hanged for Lincoln's

The box at Ford's Theatre in Washington, D.C., where President Lincoln was shot on April 14, 1865.

The hanging on July 7, 1865, of Booth's four coconspirators: Lewis Payne, David Herold, George Atzerodt, and Mary Surratt.

murder, while the others received long prison sentences, as did a doctor who treated Booth's broken leg. Surratt's son John escaped to Canada and then Britain, and was never convicted for his part in the conspiracy.

Booth's plot

Booth was the key mover in plotting the assassination. He was a fanatical racist and Confederate supporter, and from the summer of 1864 he had been scheming to kidnap Lincoln and take him to Richmond as a hostage. In March 1865 a kidnap plot was foiled by a change of presidential plans. The Confederate surrender on April 9 enraged Booth, and his fury mounted as celebrations engulfed Washington. On April 11 Booth heard President Lincoln speak from the White House in favor of limited voting rights for blacks. Appalled, Booth resolved to kill

Lincoln. When Booth visited Ford's Theatre on the morning of April 14 to pick up his mail, he overheard that the president would be attending that evening. He immediately improvised his plan and instructed Payne and Atzerodt to murder Seward and Johnson. Booth believed that such a blow to the administration would reinvigorate the Confederate cause. Instead, most Southerners shared the feelings of diarist Mary Chesnut, who wrote that "this foul murder will bring upon us worse miseries." Most Northerners felt only grief and shock. On April 25 the funeral train bearing Lincoln's body began its journey to his hometown of Springfield, Illinois. All along the 1,700-mile route people waited for hours to see the train pass. They stood with bowed heads, and at night they lit bonfires. Lincoln was buried at Oak Ridge Cemetery on May 4, 1865.

See also

- Booth, John Wilkes
- Chesnut, Mary
- Johnson, Andrew
- Lincoln, Abraham
- Reconstruction
- Seward, William H.
- Stanton, Edwin M.

Literature

The Civil War took place during the 19th-century flowering of American literature known as the American Renaissance. The cataclysmic effect of the war resulted in a huge amount of literature of varying quality being produced afterward.

One book closely associated with the Civil War, which is even said to have been a cause of the conflict, was published a decade before the first shot was fired. *Uncle Tom's Cabin*, Harriet Beecher Stowe's bestselling novel of 1852, was an indictment of the fugitive-slave laws. Her depiction of the brutalizing effects of slavery struck a chord with many readers. Critics have debated whether *Uncle Tom's Cabin* was art or abolitionist propaganda and have condemned Beecher Stowe's simplistic depiction of black characters. There is little doubt that it brought the horrors of slavery to a wider audience, especially in the North, where many people had little or no experience of slavery. It strengthened support for the abolitionist movement, deepening the divisions between North and South.

Wartime literature

Some of the earliest literary responses to the outbreak of war were popular patriotic songs. The Union had "The

A poster advertising Harriet Beecher Stowe's Uncle Tom's Cabin. *The novel was an instant success and sold 300,000 copies in its first year. It was quickly adapted into a play that was also very popular.*

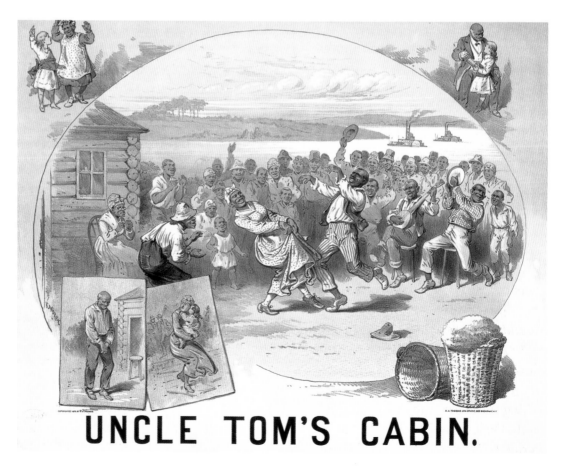

UNCLE TOM'S CABIN.

Battle-Hymn of the Republic," while the best known Confederate songs included "Maryland, My Maryland" and "The Bonnie Blue Flag."

Patriotic verses were also produced. The Quaker poet John Greenleaf Whittier wrote the well-loved pro-Union poem "Barbara Frietchie" in 1863. Whittier based his poem on a reported incident in which an old woman bravely waved her Union flag while General "Stonewall" Jackson and his Confederates were riding through Frederick, Maryland. In fact, although Barbara Frietchie was a real person, she was almost certainly not involved in any such incident. After the war Whittier achieved a national reputation with the publication of "Snow-Bound" (1866), a nostalgic poem celebrating the rural world of his native New England.

Poetry in the 1860s

During the war serious poetry was written, but much of it was not published until later. One of the most original poetic voices of the period, and indeed of the 19th century, was Walt Whitman. He produced two collections of poems during the war and made revisions and additions to his most famous work, *Leaves of Grass*, the first version of which had been published in 1855 (see box).

Also productive was James Russell Lowell, one of the finest New England poets of the 19th century, who was the first editor (1857–1861) of the *Atlantic Monthly* and coedited (1863–1872) the *North American Review* with Charles Eliot Norton.

The other leading poet who was writing throughout the Civil War was Emily Dickinson. This was her most productive period, in which she wrote

WALT WHITMAN'S CIVIL WAR

Late in 1862 the poet Walt Whitman *(below)* went to the battlefront in Virginia to find his brother George, who had been wounded at Fredericksburg while serving in the Union army. After spending some time in camp, Whitman returned to Washington, D.C., where he worked in various government departments. In his spare time he served as a volunteer nurse to soldiers of both sides who lay sick and dying in unhygienic military hospitals. He wrote letters home for them and supplied invalids with food and other necessities, which he paid for out of his own small salary.

Whitman's wartime experiences inspired two volumes of poetry: *Drum-Taps* (1865) and *Sequel to Drum-Taps* (1865–1866). The latter contains two of his most famous works—"When Lilacs Last in the Dooryard Bloom'd" and "O Captain! My Captain!" Both poems express the sadness that Walt Whitman felt on the assassination of President Abraham Lincoln. A prose volume, *Specimen Days* (1882), was an autobiographical account of Whitman's work as a nurse.

EMILY DICKINSON

Emily Elizabeth Dickinson *(below)* was one of the foremost American poets of the 19th century. She was born in Amherst, Massachusetts, on December 10, 1830. After graduating from Amherst Academy in 1847, she attended nearby Mount Holyoke Female Seminary for one year. Despite considerable pressure to become a Christian, she refused. Although many of her poems deal with God, she remained a skeptic for the rest of her life.

Dickinson began to write poetry in the 1850s. Her poems were unconventional and deceptively simple lyrics concerned with death, eternity, and the inner life. The Civil War years saw her greatest literary output: Between 1862 and 1866 she wrote more than a third of her poems. In April 1862 she wrote to the critic Thomas Wentworth Higginson asking for his opinion on her poems. Although he was impressed by their originality in form and content—irregular rhythms adapted from the meters of hymns, eccentric phrasing and syntax, and emotional intensity and candor—he advised her against publication.

By the late 1860s Dickinson had become a recluse, dressing always in white. During her final decades she never left her house and garden. Although she chose to publish only a handful of poems in her lifetime, she never doubted that her poetry would be well received. After she died in 1886, her sister decided to have her poems published. The first collection, *Poems by Emily Dickinson*, appeared in 1890. Her reputation grew gradually, and she is now regarded as one of the greatest of all poets.

some 800 poems. However, only seven of Dickinson's poems were published in her lifetime, and none at all under her own name (see box).

Relatively few works were published during the Civil War as the whole country channeled its resources into munitions and essential services. After the war, however, there was a glut of anthologies, as writers tried to come to terms with their experiences. Among the most important collections of poetry were H.H. Brownell's *War Lyrics* (1866), a book of verse by Union poets, and *War Poetry of the South* (1866), in which a well-known Southern writer, William Gilmore Simms, anthologized Confederate poems.

Merely not dying

Most of the writers who emerged in the aftermath of the Civil War were from the North, since the South was shattered culturally as well as economically. "Perhaps as you know," Southern poet Sidney Lanier wrote to a friend, "that, with us of the younger generation in the South since the War, pretty much the whole of life has been merely not dying." This feeling of hopelessness is reflected in the poetry of Henry Timrod and Paul Hamilton Hayne, who both looked back nostalgically to the prewar period. Lanier himself was the most innovative postwar Southern poet. A talented musician, he regarded verse as a "phenomenon of sound" and in *The Science of English Verse* (1880) made an extended analysis of poetics in terms of musical notation, thus anticipating many poets of the 20th century.

Memories of the war

Immediately after the war most people wanted to put the horrors of the conflict behind them and get on with their lives. However, from the 1870s there was a flood of autobiographies and reminiscences written by men from both sides, from generals to ordinary soldiers. These works are interesting historically but are not always of literary merit. Often the writers had scores to settle and wanted to put forward their version of events.

The most celebrated of the autobiographies was that by Ulysses S. Grant, the former Union general and president. Grant wrote his *Personal Memoirs* while he was suffering from throat cancer and barely managed to complete them before his death in 1885. He wrote in a straightforward, restrained, and objective style, and avoided apportioning blame. It became a classic and in a short time after his death earned Grant's family $450,000.

In the 1880s *Century* magazine published a series of hundreds of illustrated articles giving a full account of the war as experienced by those taking part, often leading generals. In

1888 these articles were collected in a four-volume set called *Battles and Leaders of the Civil War*, which is still a valuable eyewitness account of the war. There were also personal accounts by those who had worked as nurses or

An illustration from Louisa May Alcott's Little Women *(1868), showing the novel's heroine Jo and her sister Beth.*

WHITMAN'S POETRY

Extract from Walt Whitman's poem about the assassination of Abraham Lincoln, "When Lilacs Last in the Dooryard Bloom'd"

Nor for you, for one alone,
Blossoms and branches green to coffins all I bring,
For fresh as the morning, thus would I chant a song for you
O sane and sacred death.

All over bouquets of roses,
O death, I cover you over with roses and early lilies,
But mostly and now the lilac that blooms the first,
Copious I break, I break the sprigs from the bushes,
With loaded arms I come, pouring for you,
For you and the coffins all of you O death.

Stephen Crane's novel **The Red Badge of Courage** *(1895) was praised for its realistic depiction of the war, even though the author had only been born in 1867.*

See also

Virginia were narrated in black dialect. They depicted the South, both before and after the Civil War, as a society ordered by the laws of chivalry, in which the white men were noble, their women ladies, and their black slaves perfectly contented. Similarly, *Uncle Remus: His Songs and His Sayings* (1881), by Joel Chandler Harris, used folklore to evoke a romanticized past swept away by Reconstruction. These novels were popular among both nostalgic Southerners who wanted to believe that the Old South had really been such an idyllic place and Northerners who were fascinated by a world they had never known.

The influence of this style of writing, which evokes a strong sense of place, can be clearly seen in the works of Mark Twain, such as *The Adventures of Huckleberry Finn* (1884). Twain (whose real name was Samuel Clemens) had briefly joined a militia, but his main contribution to the Civil War was as the publisher of Grant's memoirs.

spies, or who simply kept a diary during the war. The novelist Louisa May Alcott (1832–1888) found fame with the publication of *Hospital Sketches* (1863), the poignant letters she wrote as a Civil War nurse in Washington, D.C. Her lasting reputation rests on the immense popularity of her semiautobiographical novel *Little Women* (1868), which follows the lives of four sisters growing up in the Civil War years.

There was a great interest in stories that took place in a particular part of the country and provided descriptions of the landscape, local customs, and dialects of a certain place. Thomas Nelson Page was a successful and much imitated writer of this kind of novel. His stories of plantation life in

Later works

The first major work of fiction about the Civil War by an author who was born after the end of the conflict was *The Red Badge of Courage* (1895), by Stephen Crane. The novel was praised for its harrowing realism and vivid depictions of battle scenes. The other most celebrated literary work about the Civil War is *Gone with the Wind* (1936), the only novel by Margaret Mitchell. This 1,000-page Pulitzer Prize-winning romance about the destruction of the Old South during the Civil War became the bestselling novel in U.S. history and the basis for a film in 1939 that is among the most famous movies ever made.

Longstreet, James

James Longstreet (1821–1904) was an able Confederate general who went on to become a political ally of President Ulysses S. Grant. He was unpopular in the postwar South, and his battlefield decisions were often criticized.

Longstreet was born in 1821 in South Carolina, but his family moved to Georgia when he was very young. Longstreet graduated from the U.S. Military Academy at West Point in 1842 and fought in the Mexican War (1846–1848), where he was wounded. At the outbreak of the Civil War Longstreet resigned from the U.S. Army and headed to Richmond, where he was commissioned brigadier general in the Confederate army.

Longstreet was assigned to the staff of General Pierre G.T. Beauregard and fought in the First Battle of Bull Run (Manassas) in July 1861. At Second Bull Run on August 29–30, 1862, Longstreet was slow to attack at first but distinguished himself with a ferocious counterattack that shattered the Union army on August 30.

Corps command

Following the Battle of Antietam (Sharpsburg) on September 17, 1862, Longstreet was promoted to lieutenant general and given command of I Corps in General Robert E. Lee's Army of Northern Virginia. In that capacity he took part in the Confederate victory at Fredericksburg on December 13, 1862, and the decisive Confederate defeat at Gettysburg in July 1863. Longstreet went on to receive a severe shoulder wound in the Wilderness Campaign in May 1864, but returned to command

James Longstreet, pictured in civilian clothes after the war. Longstreet joined the Republican Party and was appointed U.S. ambassador to Turkey (1880–1881) by President Grant.

with a paralyzed arm and surrendered with Lee at Appomattox in April 1865.

After the war Longstreet was disliked in the South because he joined the Republican Party and accepted a succession of appointments from president and former Union general Ulysses S. Grant. Many Southerners also blamed Longstreet for the defeat at Gettysburg, in particular for his delay in making an attack on July 2. Longstreet spent his later years back in Georgia, where he ran a hotel and raised turkeys. In 1896 he published his memoirs, which defended his actions at Gettysburg. Longstreet died in 1904.

See also

- Bull Run (Manassas), Second Battle of
- Early, Jubal A.
- Fredericksburg, Battle of
- Gettysburg, Battle of
- Grant, Ulysses S.
- Northern Virginia, Army of
- Republican Party

Lost Cause

The Lost Cause was a particular set of beliefs about the causes and events of the Civil War that idealized life in the prewar Old South and explained, in a way that Southerners found acceptable, how the Confederacy lost the war.

The Lost Cause myth developed among Southerners trying to come to terms with a shattering defeat, giving them a way in which they could retain their self-respect. The phrase "Lost Cause" was first used by Edward A. Pollard as the title of his 1866 history, which presented the Confederacy as a valiant institution brought low by an unfeeling enemy. It became a shorthand expression for the South's collective memory of what the Old South had stood for and the sacrifices it had made in the defense of its unique way of life.

Key beliefs

There were several key beliefs in the creation of the Lost Cause myth. One was that slavery had not been the cause of the war. It was just a smokescreen for the North's unprovoked aggression against the South. Rather, the war was a struggle for states' rights, in which secession was the only honorable response to an enemy who was bent on oppression. Far from being rebels, the Southerners were American patriots, the true defenders of the Constitution. Those who believed in the Lost Cause refused to acknowledge that slavery had been a terrible abuse of human rights, or that the transition from a slave society to a free-labor society was an advance. They developed a vision of the Old South as an idyllic rural society in which humane masters had lived in harmony with contented slaves. Popular novels by writers such as Thomas N. Page reinforced this idea.

Another key Lost Cause theme was that Confederate defeat had been inevitable from the outset because the South faced impossible odds. According to this version of events, the North's overwhelming superiority in terms of manpower and material wealth—especially industrial capacity—was bound to prevail despite the fact that the Confederacy had the better leaders and the braver soldiers. The Confederate generals Robert E. Lee and Thomas "Stonewall" Jackson were venerated almost as saints. The sacrifices of the dead and veteran soldiers were constantly remembered

Giant sculptures of three great heroes of Lost Cause mythology: Confederate President Jefferson Davis and generals Robert E. Lee and "Stonewall" Jackson, carved on Stone Mountain, Atlanta, Georgia.

with special holidays, monuments, and the setting up of patriotic organizations. All these activities saw the Lost Cause myth being developed and reinforced.

Role in Reconstruction

The Lost Cause myth played a significant part in the way the former Confederate states developed after the war. For one thing, it gave a justification for the terrorist activities of racist organizations such as the Ku Klux Klan. For those who did not accept the result of the war and the end of slavery, the Klansmen were freedom fighters defending decent citizens against interfering Northerners and dangerous former slaves. Once the federal troops left in 1877 and Southerners could again regulate relations between blacks and whites, the Lost Cause myth comfortably fit the creation of a racially segregated society. The rights of African Americans were gradually suppressed in the last decades of the 19th century.

National reconciliation

At first the Northerners considered the Southerners' refusal to accept defeat arrogant, but gradually they began to acknowledge the sacrifices of the South. For the sake of reconciliation and reunion the heroism of the soldiers of both sides was emphasized, rather than the root causes of the war. By the beginning of the 20th century Civil War commemorations had taken on a national flavor.

The Lost Cause version of events became more acceptable. People on both sides of the Mason–Dixon line flocked to see D. W. Griffith's silent movie *Birth of a Nation* (1915), which put a favorable gloss on Southern resistance to Reconstruction and

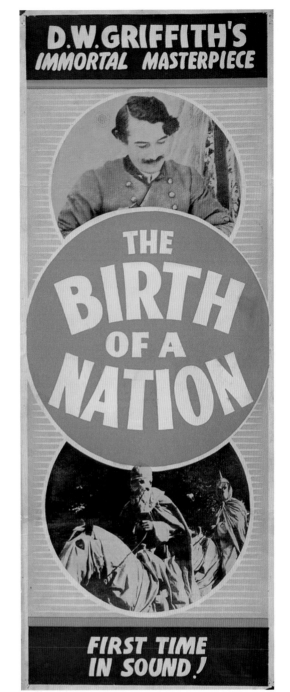

A poster advertising D.W. Griffith's epic 1915 movie **Birth of a Nation**, *which romanticized the Ku Klux Klan and included many Lost Cause themes, such as the idea that slavery was not the true cause of the war, and that emancipation had been a disaster.*

presented the Ku Klux Klan in a positive light. Margaret Mitchell's bestselling novel *Gone With the Wind* (1936) became a hugely successful movie. The storyline was another version of the Lost Cause myth, a soft-focus look at plantation life.

The civil rights struggles of the 1950s and 1960s witnessed perhaps the last outpouring of Lost Cause sentiments, since many who resisted civil rights justified their stance in language reminiscent of the Lost Cause myth.

See also

- Causes of the conflict
- Ku Klux Klan
- Lee, Robert E.
- Legacy of the Civil War
- Literature
- Memorials and souvenirs
- Movies
- Propaganda
- Race and racism
- Reconstruction
- Slavery

Louisiana

Louisiana played a major role in the events of the Civil War, from the secession crisis that started the war to some of the first experiments with Reconstruction policy. In between, it was the scene of several critical battles and campaigns.

In its ethnic makeup Louisiana was the most diverse state in the Confederacy. In 1860 the state had a population of nearly 710,000. The south of the state was one of the country's richest agricultural regions, dominated by wealthy planters who grew sugar cane using slave labor. Also living in southern Louisiana was a large population of French-speaking Cajuns, whose ancestors had emigrated there from French Canada a century earlier. Most were small farmers, fishermen, or trappers. Anglo-Americans who had emigrated from the older Southern states dominated northern Louisiana, where they grew cotton and raised livestock. New Orleans was the largest city in the Deep South, with nearly 170,000 inhabitants. It had the most European immigrants in the South, in addition to many Northern-born business and professional people. There were 332,000 slaves, making up 47 percent of the state's population. This diversity created divided loyalties before, during, and after the war.

The Whig Party had been very strong in state politics in the 1850s, supported especially by sugar planters and businesspeople. Former Whigs and many immigrants opposed secession. In the 1860 election 55 percent voted for John Bell or Stephen A. Douglas, both of whom were Unionists. Although secessionists accounted for only 50 of the 130 delegates to the state secession convention, secession was eventually carried by 117 votes to 13.

Capture of New Orleans

The most important military action in Louisiana took place in April 1862, just a year into the war. Governor Thomas O. Moore had allowed most of the state's soldiers to be sent outside the state. Officials knew that any Union attack would come up the Mississippi River from the Gulf of Mexico, but they believed that Forts Jackson and St. Philip, which lay on opposite sides of the river south of New Orleans, would protect the city. However, a Union fleet commanded by David G. Farragut bombarded the forts and then steamed

Southern Louisiana's rich farmland was used for growing sugar cane. The slave-produced crop was the source of much of the state's wealth.

At the Battle of Baton Rouge on August 5, 1862, Confederate forces attacked Baton Rouge, the capital of Louisiana, held by Union forces since May, but failed to retake the city.

past them on April 24, taking New Orleans on April 29 with little opposition. The loss of New Orleans badly damaged the Confederacy. The South lost not only its busiest port but also one of its biggest iron foundries, critical shipbuilding facilities, and its major banking center. Farragut's victory also dealt a blow to Confederate morale. By early summer Union troops had captured the state capital, Baton Rouge, and most of southern Louisiana.

Union occupation

Benjamin F. Butler, the Union military governor of New Orleans, soon found that despite the many Unionists in Louisiana, the people of New Orleans and the surrounding area deeply resented Union occupation. He hanged a man who lowered the U.S. flag that flew over the mint in New Orleans. When local women showed disrespect for Union troops, he issued his infamous "woman order," which declared that any woman failing to

respect Union soldiers would be treated as a prostitute. For these actions he was given the nickname "Beast" Butler.

Confederate counterattack

A Confederate counterattack under Richard Taylor returned much of the sugar-planting region to Confederate control in spring 1863, but the achievement was shortlived. On July 9 Union troops commanded by Nathaniel P. Banks captured Port Hudson on the Mississippi, and Taylor was forced to give up most of his earlier gains. The fall of Port Hudson, coming just five days after the capture of Vicksburg, gave the Union control of the entire Mississippi River.

Port Hudson was also important for being the first battle in which black troops saw large-scale action against white Confederates. The black infantry companies raised by Butler in New Orleans performed valiantly and convinced many white Northerners that African Americans were good soldiers.

Union sailors in a rowboat confront a crowd in New Orleans on April 25, 1862. The Union fleet had sailed past the two forts protecting New Orleans the previous day, so the city's surrender was inevitable. New Orleans fell to the Union on April 29.

The last major campaign of the war in Louisiana came in spring 1864, when Banks mounted a major campaign up the Red River to Shreveport and then into northeast Texas. However, a Confederate counterattack in early April forced Banks to retreat to the Mississippi, so Louisiana never came fully under Union control.

Effects of the war

The war brought great destruction to southern Louisiana, as plantations were burned, animals confiscated, and planting disrupted. Since slaves greatly outnumbered whites in many of the plantation regions, Union commanders had to decide what to do with slaves in areas under their control. Banks declared slavery "void" in occupied Louisiana, but he then decided to make the former slaves stay on the plantations and work for wages. Abolitionists pointed out that forced labor was little different from slavery.

In 1864 Louisiana became a political testing ground for Reconstruction. Between April and July a convention met and wrote a new state constitution that abolished slavery and opened public schools and the court system to African Americans. This complied with President Lincoln's terms. But Congress, dominated by Radical Republicans, distrusted the former Confederates and wanted the state to guarantee the civil rights of the freed slaves. As a result of this disagreement, Congress rejected the state's representatives and electoral votes in the national elections of 1864.

In all, 56,000 Louisianans served in the Confederate army, and 7,000 died. Another 10,000 served in home guard units. Roughly 24,000 African Americans and 2,400 whites from Louisiana fought for the Union. The state lost more than half of its prewar wealth and took decades to recover from the devastation of the war.

McClellan, George B.

George Brinton McClellan (1826–1885) rose quickly to take overall command of the Union army. He successfully created an effective fighting force from raw recruits, but his lack of decisiveness made him a poor battlefield commander.

McClellan was born in 1826 in Philadelphia. After he graduated second in his class from the U.S. Military Academy at West Point at the young age of 20, his future looked bright. He was immediately able to make his mark in the Mexican War (1846–1848). After that he returned to West Point to teach engineering and from 1851 onward to conduct surveys for the construction of military installations. In 1855 the army sent McClellan as an official observer to the Crimean War (1853–1856) in Russia, where he was able to observe European methods of warfare at first hand. Frustrated with his slow progress within the army establishment, however, the intensely ambitious McClellan resigned his commission in 1857 to became chief of engineering for the Illinois Central Railroad. By the time the Civil War began in 1861, he was president of the Ohio and Mississippi Railroad.

Return to the army

At the outbreak of the war McClellan joined the Ohio Volunteers and in May 1861 was appointed a major general in the regular army (he had left it four years earlier as a mere captain). As commander of Union forces in the Ohio Valley, his instructions were to hold on to western Virginia (later West Virginia) for the Union. He secured the region by mid-July, having encountered little resistance, and was soon being talked up in newspapers as the "Young Napoleon of the West."

In the wake of the Union rout at First Bull Run at the end of July 1861 McClellan seemed the obvious choice to replace McDowell in command of the demoralized Union troops south of the Potomac. Not content with the responsibility for defending Washington, D.C., McClellan began undermining the elderly general-in-chief of the army, Winfield Scott. With the press and an adoring public behind him, by November 1861 he had managed to elbow Scott aside. So in just a few short months the young ex-captain had risen to command the entire U.S. Army.

General-in-chief

McClellan very quickly demonstrated the mixture of positive and negative qualities that would make him such a baffling figure. His first achievement was to create, name, and organize the Army of the Potomac. Throughout the winter of 1861–62 he put in 18-hour

General George B. McClellan at the height of his career. He was popular with the public, and there was widespread disbelief in the North when Lincoln removed him from command in late 1862.

enemy in battle. It was not until April 1862 that Lincoln was able to persuade McClellan to send the Army of the Potomac out to fight. At one point an exasperated Lincoln wrote a note in which he said that if McClellan was not using the army, "I should like to borrow it for a while."

Unfit for command

When McClellan finally did commit his army to real fighting, he proved unfit for battlefield command. Throughout the Peninsular Campaign (April–July 1862) he made repeated calls for reinforcements despite vastly outnumbering the enemy at every step. After the Union defeat at the Second Battle of Bull Run (August 1862) McClellan had the great good fortune to have Confederate General Robert E. Lee's battle plan for Antietam (Sharpsburg) fall into his hands. Even with that valuable information he could manage no more than an inconclusive result in the battle (September 1862). His failure to pursue the defeated Confederates in the aftermath of Antietam seemed to demonstrate his lack of stomach for battle and gave the president the excuse he needed to strip McClellan of command.

Political career

McClellan was sidelined for the rest of the war. He tried his hand at politics, typically starting at the top by challenging Lincoln for the presidency as the Democratic candidate in the election of 1864. McClellan was heavily defeated and resigned from the army the same day. At the end of the 1870s McClellan served as governor of New Jersey, then spent his time traveling and writing. He died in 1885.

A banner for the 1864 election in which McClellan (left) was the Democratic candidate opposing Lincoln.

See also

- Antietam (Sharpsburg), Battle of
- Democratic Party
- Election of 1864
- Lincoln, Abraham
- Peninsular Campaign
- Potomac, Army of the
- Union army

days drilling troops and boosting morale. In this role he demonstrated an almost comical self-importance, revealed in letters to his wife. "You have no idea how the men brighten up now when I go among them … I believe they love me…. God has placed a great work in my hands." While puffing himself up, he was scathing about the entire civilian administration, including President Abraham Lincoln, whom he dismissed as "the original gorilla."

More serious than his big-headedness, though, was McClellan's strange reluctance to use the superb army he had created to confront the

McDowell, Irvin

General Irvin McDowell (1818–1885) was one of the least successful Union commanders. He led the Union army to defeat in the first battle of the war, at Bull Run (Manassas) on July 21, 1861, and was then relegated to corps command.

McDowell was born in Ohio in 1818. He spent his childhood in France and then returned to the United States, where he graduated from the U.S. Military Academy at West Point in 1838. During the Mexican War (1846–1848) he was commended for bravery. When the Civil War began, McDowell was at U.S. Army headquarters in Washington, D.C. He was appointed brigadier general and given command of the Union troops south of the Potomac. It therefore fell to McDowell to command Union forces in the first major battle of the war, at Bull Run (Manassas) in Virginia on July 21, 1861. The Confederates scattered Union troops and forced them to retreat back to Washington.

Defending Washington
Days after the defeat at First Bull Run McDowell was relegated to corps command and replaced by Major General George B. McClellan, who energetically set about organizing the Army of the Potomac. McDowell was given command of I Corps and charged with defending Washington while McClellan embarked on the Peninsular Campaign (April–July 1862). By early July the Confederates had turned back McClellan's attempt to capture Richmond. Confederate General Robert E. Lee then turned his attention north to target Union forces under General John Pope, which included McDowell's corps. On August 29–30 the corps took part in a second battle at Bull Run Creek, which turned into a Union disaster. McDowell commanded the largest corps at the Second Battle of Bull Run (Manassas), and he came under severe criticism for failing to make effective use of his large force.

The end of McDowell's career
After Second Bull Run, in which the Union lost 16,000 men compared with 9,200 Confederate casualties, McDowell faced accusations of having failed in command. Although a court of inquiry cleared him, his career in the field was over. For the next two years he had desk duties with the promotion board in Washington and from 1864 was sent west to command the defenses of the Pacific Coast. McDowell continued to hold high positions in the U.S. Army for some years after the war. He spent his last working years as a park commissioner in San Francisco and died in 1885.

Irvin McDowell attended a military school in France as a boy before entering the U.S. Military Academy at West Point in 1834.

See also
- Bull Run (Manassas), First Battle of
- Bull Run (Manassas), Second Battle of
- McClellan, George B.
- Peninsular Campaign
- Pope, John
- Potomac, Army of the

25

McPherson, James

McPherson (1828–1864) became the highest-ranking Union officer to die in Civil War combat when he was shot at the Battle of Atlanta in July 1864. McPherson had risen to be an able corps commander in the Army of the Tennessee.

McPherson was born into a poor family near Clyde, Ohio, in 1828. He attended the U.S. Military Academy at West Point, graduating first in his class in 1853. John Bell Hood, a future Confederate general, was a great friend of his in the same class. Hood was on the opposite side at the Battle of Atlanta, where McPherson was killed.

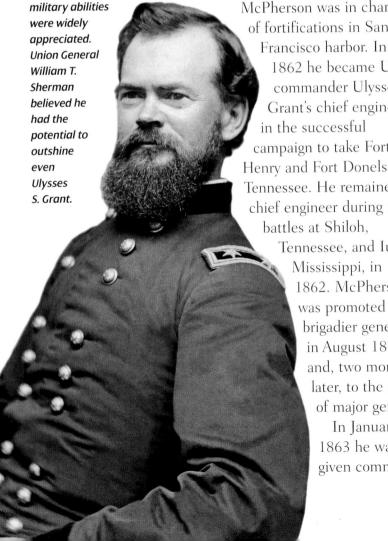

James McPherson's military abilities were widely appreciated. Union General William T. Sherman believed he had the potential to outshine even Ulysses S. Grant.

Grant's chief engineer

When war broke out in 1861, McPherson was in charge of fortifications in San Francisco harbor. In 1862 he became Union commander Ulysses S. Grant's chief engineer in the successful campaign to take Fort Henry and Fort Donelson, Tennessee. He remained chief engineer during the battles at Shiloh, Tennessee, and Iuka, Mississippi, in 1862. McPherson was promoted to brigadier general in August 1862 and, two months later, to the rank of major general. In January 1863 he was given command of XVII Corps in the Army of the Tennessee. His corps played a central role in the campaign to take the Mississippi port of Vicksburg.

Atlanta campaign

On March 12, 1864, McPherson took command of the Army of the Tennessee. For the last 10 weeks of his life, in spring and summer 1864, McPherson took part in Sherman's Atlanta campaign through northern Georgia. McPherson's 24,000-strong army made up Sherman's right flank, with the Armies of the Cumberland and the Ohio on the left flank. They drove Joseph E. Johnston's Confederate forces south to Atlanta. Sherman was irritated at McPherson's caution when he failed to attack the rear of the Confederate army at Snake Creek Gap, but McPherson felt he needed more troops to accomplish the task. Later in the campaign Sherman repeatedly used McPherson's army to outflank strong Confederate defensive positions.

During the Battle of Atlanta, when Union and Confederate armies clashed to the east of the city on July 22, 1864, McPherson was shot in the back. The ball punctured his lung and passed out of his chest, and he died soon afterward. Sherman said: "McPherson's death was a great loss to me." Grant added: "A nation grieves at the loss of one so dear to our nation's cause."

Maine

One of the staunchest bastions of the Union with a strong antislavery tradition, Maine sent large numbers of men to serve in the Union armies and supplied large quantities of equipment and provisions to the war effort.

Maine entered the Union as a free state in March 1820 as part of the Missouri Compromise, balancing Missouri's entry as a slave state. By 1860 the state had a population of nearly 630,000. Many people in Maine supported abolition, and Harriet Beecher Stowe wrote her bestselling antislavery novel *Uncle Tom's Cabin* while living there. In the 1860 presidential election the state's citizens voted overwhelmingly for Abraham Lincoln, partly because they supported what they took to be his abolitionist objectives, and partly because his running mate, Hannibal Hamlin, was a native of the state.

The outbreak of the Civil War was greeted with enthusiasm in Maine. Many men volunteered immediately, and in total Maine supplied 67,000 soldiers to the Union army. The state suffered almost 20,000 casualties, of whom 9,000 died.

Famous soldiers from Maine

One of the most famous Maine soldiers was Major General Oliver O. Howard, who distinguished himself at Seven Pines and commanded the Union Army of the Tennessee during William T. Sherman's march through Georgia and the Carolinas. After the war Howard took charge of the Freedmen's Bureau. He was one of the founders of Howard University in Washington, D.C. Perhaps the most famous of Maine's soldiers was Joshua L. Chamberlain. He fought battles from Antietam to Appomattox, where he was one of the soldiers who accepted the Confederate surrender. He later served four terms as governor of Maine, then became president of Bowdoin College.

Staunch supporters

As the war dragged on, enthusiasm for it dropped, especially among shipbuilders and merchants, many of whose vessels had been sunk by Confederate commerce raiders, and among those who worked in the transatlantic cotton trade, which had been severely disrupted. Most Maine residents, however, remained firmly behind the cause from start to finish.

See also

- Abolition
- Chamberlain, Joshua L.
- Freedmen's Bureau
- Gettysburg, Battle of
- Missouri Compromise
- Stowe, Harriet Beecher, and *Uncle Tom's Cabin*

A view of the city hall and market square in Portland, Maine, in 1853. Portland was the state capital until 1832, when Augusta became the capital.

Maps and plans

Before the Civil War much of the United States was unmapped. Those maps that existed were often inaccurate or out of date. When war broke out in 1861, there was a desperate need to obtain reliable maps of the territory.

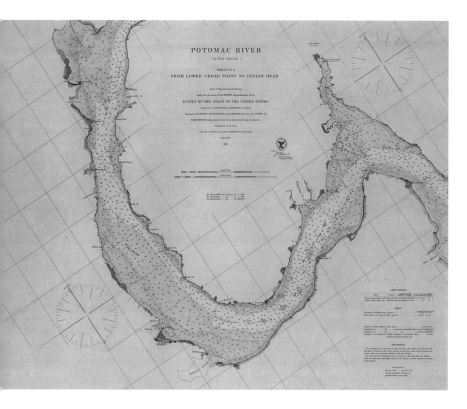

The Potomac River from Lower Cedar Point to Indian Head. The U.S. Coast Survey produced this map for the Union in 1862. Knowledge of the Potomac was critical for the defense of Washington, D.C.

In order to plan the movements of their armies, Union and Confederate generals needed detailed information about terrain, river crossings, roads, and even houses, barns, and fences. During the Peninsular Campaign in Virginia in spring 1862 Union General George B. McClellan lamented that "correct local maps were not to be found … erroneous courses to streams and roads were frequently given."

Both armies had trained mapmakers, known as topographical engineers, although the Union men had better surveying equipment. The Union also expanded the mapping work of the U.S.

Coast Survey. In 1862 the Coast Survey printed 44,000 maps for military purposes—five times the number it produced in a typical prewar year.

When there was no time to have a map made and printed in advance, army topographers produced maps while accompanying troops on the move. At first field maps were hand-traced onto thin linen to produce copies. Later, topographers also photographed maps to make copies more quickly. The copies were cut and mounted on cloth so they could be folded and fit in a pocket or saddlebag.

In enemy range

Civil War topographers often acted as reconnaissance officers as well as surveyors. They rode out a long way in front of the army to produce maps of the area ahead, and that brought them close to the enemy. They used that vantage point to make plans of the enemy's positions and fortifications, although working in sight and range of the opposing side was dangerous.

A few Civil War maps were sketched from balloon. Aeronaut John La Montain made one of the earliest such sketches on August 10, 1861, showing the location of Confederate tents and batteries at Sewall's Point, Virginia.

It was also the mapmaker's task to compile maps for battle reports. To do this, they had to liaise with divisional and corps officers after the battle to discover the exact positions of the different units during the fighting. We owe to their work much of our detailed knowledge of troop deployments in Civil War battles.

Jedediah Hotchkiss

One of the most successful topographers was a Confederate, Jedediah Hotchkiss. On March 26, 1862, he joined General Thomas "Stonewall" Jackson in the Shenandoah Valley. Jackson's description of his role was brief and to the point: "I want you to make me a map of the Valley, from

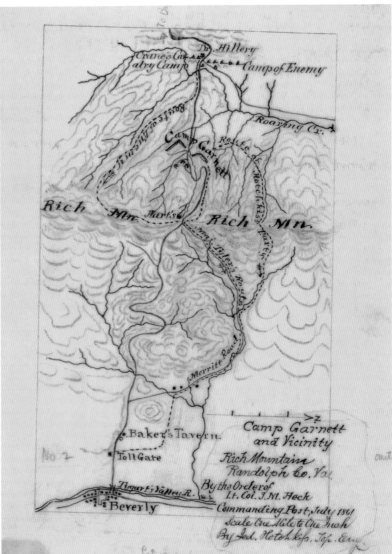

TOPOGRAPHER'S JOURNAL

Mapmaker Jedediah Hotchkiss made the following journal entry on May 8, 1862.

"The General [Jackson] sent me in advance with skirmishers, up the winding turnpike road along an eastward spur of Bullpasture Mountain, and when, at each turn of the road, I found the way clear I waved my handkerchief, then he came on with the main column. ... Having reached the summit I took General Jackson out to the right of the gap to the end of a rocky spur overlooking the Bullpasture Valley, and showed him the enemy in position near McDowell. At the same time, as he looked on, I made him a map of McDowell and vicinity, showing the enemy's position, as in full view before us. ... I [then] rode with Generals Jackson and Johnson across the field on the crest of the mountain, to reconnoiter. Discovering us, the enemy's skirmishers advanced from the Bullpasture Valley, fired on us and forced us to retire."

Harpers Ferry to Lexington, showing all the points of offense and defense in those places." In the next three months Hotchkiss kept up a continual reconnaissance of the valley. He is credited with helping Jackson win the Valley Campaign (March–June 1862), in which Jackson's men covered 670 miles (1,070km) and fought five battles. Hotchkiss continued to work with Jackson after the campaign. At the Battle of Chancellorsville in May 1863 he found a route for Jackson's corps through dense woods, which enabled them to launch a flank attack on the Union and win the battle.

A map showing Union and Confederate positions at Rich Mountain, Virginia. The sketch map was made by Confederate topographer Jedediah Hotchkiss in July 1861.

See also

- Chancellorsville, Battle of
- Jackson, Thomas J.
- Reconnaissance
- Shenandoah Valley
- Strategy and tactics

March to the Sea and the Carolinas Campaign

In late 1864 Union General William T. Sherman led his troops on a destructive march through Georgia to the sea and then north through the Carolinas. This demonstration of strength was one of the most famous episodes of the war.

Scenes depicting events from Sherman's March to the Sea through Georgia, published in Harper's Weekly *in 1864.*

Following his capture of Atlanta, Georgia, on September 3, 1864, Union General William T. Sherman rested his army and planned his next move. His supply line, the railroad from Chattanooga, Tennessee, was under constant attack by the Confederate Army of Tennessee. After several weeks trying to protect the railroad, Sherman realized it was an impossible task. He decided instead to march to Savannah, a port on the Atlantic Coast 220 miles (352km) away. On the march his men would live off the land. The capture of Savannah would enable Union ships to supply the army and give Sherman a secure base from which to operate.

Sherman also hoped that the march would strike a psychological blow to the Confederacy. He wrote of the plan to Ulysses S. Grant, "If we can march a well-appointed army right through [Confederate] territory, it is a demonstration ... that we have a power which [Jefferson] Davis cannot resist." On the way his troops would cut supply lines and "smash things generally." Sherman was an advocate of total war. He argued that to win, the Union had to break the South's will to resist by making "old and young, rich and poor, feel the hard hand of war."

A daring plan

Abandoning the supply line was risky, but Sherman was confident that Georgia farms produced more than enough to feed his troops. There was also a second risk. Sherman intended to turn away from the Confederate Army

HARPER'S WEEKLY. [JULY 2, 1864.

RAILROAD DEPOT AT RESACA, GEORGIA.

ADAIRSVILLE, GEORGIA.

KINGSTON, GEORGIA.

WOODLANDS, GEORGIA.

BURNING THE RAILROAD BRIDGE AT RESACA.

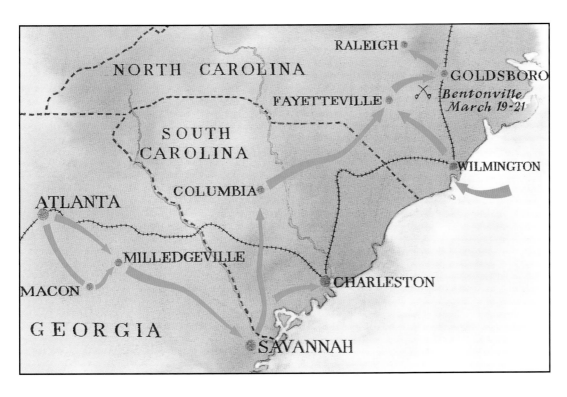

Between November 15, 1864, and March 25, 1865, Union troops marched 600 miles (960km) through Georgia and the Carolinas. The marches showed how weak the Confederacy had become, and their destructiveness demoralized the Southern people.

of Tennessee, leaving it free to try and invade Union-occupied Tennessee. To counter this threat, Sherman sent 35,000 troops back to defend Nashville in November 1864. Then he burned everything of military value in Atlanta—about one-third of the city accidentally burned as well—and on November 15 set out with 60,000 men to Savannah.

Unopposed march

As Sherman's men headed southeast, the Confederates turned back to Tennessee as predicted to embark on an ill-fated invasion. This left no forces to oppose Sherman except Confederate cavalry and Georgia militia. As a result, Sherman was able to spread his army along a path 60 miles (96km) wide. By moving in such a dispersed pattern, his army greatly eased the task of supplying itself from the countryside. Parties of foragers set forth each day to scour the land for pork, beef, corn, and other foods. As the troops advanced, they paused regularly to wreck railroads and

burn factories, cotton gins, and anything else that might be valuable to the Confederate war effort. In many cases the authorized foraging was accompanied by theft and vandalism, officially deplored but unofficially tolerated. There were also thousands of lawless stragglers following the army, who were beyond military control. Even some of Sherman's battle-hardened men voiced misgivings about the harsh treatment of civilians.

Some of the most badly treated Southerners were the African American slaves liberated by the Union army. On one occasion a Union general burned a bridge over a creek to prevent any African Americans from following. He did so knowing that the Confederate cavalry was just a short distance away. Hundreds of slaves found their path to freedom blocked, and some drowned trying to swim the stream and escape.

Sherman captured Savannah on December 21, 1864. His next move was to join forces with Ulysses S. Grant

A Northern engraving showing former slaves following the Union army during the March to the Sea in late 1864.

in Virginia and defeat Robert E. Lee's army on the Richmond–Petersburg front. Sherman considered moving his troops by sea from Savannah but then determined on a second march through the Carolinas. The march began on February 1, 1865.

Sherman in the Carolinas
This march was more challenging than the first. There were more Confederate troops obstructing Sherman's advance, as well as several swampy rivers. Winter rains had turned the roads to mud. Nevertheless the Union troops surprised the Confederate command with the speed of their advance.

The destruction in South Carolina was much more widespread than in Georgia. This time the targets for pillaging and burning included towns and homes. South Carolina had been the first state to secede and was seen by many Union soldiers as responsible for the war. For this, Sherman wrote, "the whole army is burning with an insatiable desire to wreak vengeance on South Carolina." The worst single event was the burning of Columbia, the state capital, on February 17–18, 1865, although whether it was Union troops or retreating Confederates who started the fire remains a matter of controversy.

By early March Sherman's army had crossed into North Carolina. Joseph E. Johnston's Confederates tried to stop its progress at Bentonville on March 19–21, but failed. A few days later Sherman occupied Raleigh, the state capital. Within weeks the war was over. Johnston surrendered to Sherman on April 26. Sherman's marches through Georgia and the Carolinas had been decisive. They showed how weak the Confederacy had become, while their destructiveness demoralized the population and hastened its defeat.

SHERMAN'S TROOPS IN COLUMBIA

Emma LeConte, a girl living in Columbia, South Carolina, when Sherman's troops occupied the city on February 17–18, 1865, describes her experience:

"At about seven o'clock ... Henry told me there was a fire on Main Street. Sumter Street was brightly lighted by a burning house so near our piazza that we could feel the heat. By the red glare we could watch the wretches walking—generally staggering—back and forth from the camp to the town—shouting—hurrahing—cursing South Carolina—swearing—blaspheming—singing ribald songs and using obscene language. ... The drunken devils roamed about setting fire to every house the flames seemed likely to spare. ... They would enter houses and in the presence of helpless women and children, pour turpentine on the beds and set them on fire. ... The wind blew a fearful gale, wafting the flames from house to house with frightful rapidity. By midnight the whole town (except the outskirts) was wrapped in one huge blaze."

Maryland

Although Maryland is a small state, its strategic location on the border between the Union and the Confederacy made it critically important in the Civil War. Both sides realized this, and the state was the scene of much conflict.

Maryland was a slave state, but by 1860 slavery was less important there than in most other states. In 1860 there were only 87,000 slaves in Maryland, compared with 84,000 free blacks and 516,000 whites. The northern, central, and western parts of Maryland were generally loyal to the Union. However, there were many secessionists in the southern and eastern parts of the state. They were a source of great concern for President Abraham Lincoln. His problem was that Maryland completely surrounded all northern routes to Washington, D.C. If Maryland seceded or was taken over by the Confederacy, the capital of the United States would be cut off from the rest of the North and might have to be abandoned. That would signal to the world that the Union could not put down the rebellion, thus striking a disastrous blow to the Union's chances of winning the war.

Pro-South riots

Lincoln was awakened to the problem that Maryland posed on April 19, 1861, when the 6th Massachusetts Regiment was attacked by an angry mob as it marched through Baltimore on its way to Washington, D.C. Lincoln responded by suspending the writ of habeas corpus, thus allowing Union army officers to arrest suspected Confederate sympathizers and keep them in jail indefinitely without putting them on trial. Prosecession newspapers were censored. Lincoln basically had to keep Maryland in the Union by force.

Military battleground

Maryland had been a political battleground from the start of the war, but in September 1862 it became a military battleground. After his victory at the Second Battle of Bull Run (Manassas) in Virginia in August 1862 Confederate General Robert E. Lee decided to invade the state. Lee hoped that his army's presence in Maryland would cause the state to secede. It was also harvest time, and he wanted to feed his hungry army from Union fields

The citizens of Baltimore, Maryland, build barricades on hearing the news of Confederate General Robert E. Lee's advance into Pennsylvania in June 1863.

A view of the small town of Sharpsburg, Maryland, which became the scene of the war's bloodiest day when the Battle of Antietam took place on September 17, 1862.

Creek near the town of Sharpsburg, Lee had managed to get most of his army back together. The battle that followed on September 17 was the bloodiest day of the war. McClellan lost more than 12,400 men either killed, wounded, or missing. Lee's army, which had suffered 10,000 casualties, was too crippled to continue the fight, so the Confederates retreated to Virginia.

The tide turns

After the Battle of Antietam Maryland became more committed to the Union cause. Marylanders had seen the Confederate army fail, and Lincoln was continuing his crackdown on disloyalty. Lee's troops briefly passed through Maryland again in 1863 on their way to Pennsylvania and the disastrous Battle of Gettysburg, and again on their retreat after the battle. The tide of public opinion was turning against the Confederacy in the state, however, and by 1864 there was serious discussion of abolishing slavery. That summer Confederate General Jubal A. Early conducted a destructive raid in western Maryland. Although he was soon forced to retreat, his actions turned even more of the state's citizens against the war.

On October 13, 1864, the voters of Maryland narrowly approved a new state constitution abolishing slavery. Knowing that slavery was nearing an end, many slaveholders made their slaves sign labor contracts forcing them to continue to work on the plantations after emancipation. Lincoln carried the state in the November 1864 election, further cementing Maryland's ties to the Union. By the end of the war most Marylanders had seen enough of war and were ready for peace.

and storehouses. Finally, military success on Union soil would strike a blow to Northern morale and send a signal to foreign powers that the Confederacy could hold its own. Then, perhaps, European nations would recognize the independence of the Confederacy and provide aid.

Confederate invasion

Lee crossed the Potomac River into Maryland 35 miles (56km) above Washington on September 4, 1862. At Frederick he divided his army—a risky undertaking that went against traditional military thinking. To make matters worse for Lee, Union soldiers found a copy of his plans wrapped around a bundle of cigars that a Confederate soldier had accidentally dropped. Union General George B. McClellan knew exactly what Lee was doing. Still, McClellan did not move quickly. By the time the two armies faced one another along Antietam

Mascots

Keeping animals as mascots was popular among army units of North and South. A surprising variety of animals were adopted. The animals lived in camp, traveled with the men on the march, and shared the hardships and dangers.

The presence of an animal mascot in the ranks came to identify many regiments as clearly as their regimental colors. Some mascots came to be looked on as semiofficial members of the unit. Dogs were the most widely kept mascots, for their loyalty and hardiness. Care and welfare of these animals often proved important to the morale of the soldiers.

Pets and strays

Many animal mascots began their army lives as pets kept by individual soldiers or as strays that wandered into camp. The 11th Pennsylvania, for example, adopted a Staffordshire bull terrier called Sallie, which had been given to one of its officers as a puppy. She stayed with the regiment through much of its war service and was wounded once by enemy action. Sallie was with the Union men at Gettysburg in July 1863, but was killed in February 1865 during the Battle of Hatcher's Run, Virginia, and was buried on the battlefield. The soldiers of the 11th Pennsylvania felt the loss so deeply that an image of Sallie appears on the 11th Pennsylvania's memorial, which stands on the Gettysburg battlefield site.

The monument to the Union Irish Brigade at Gettysburg features an Irish wolfhound, which was the mascot of the 69th New York. The regiment adopted two of these dogs during the

war. On dress parade days the dogs were decked out in specially made green coats. An image of a wolfhound also appeared on the regimental flag.

Captured mascots

Some dog mascots followed their regiments into captivity. Frank, the mascot of the 2nd Kentucky, went into prison when the regiment was captured at Fort Donelson, Tennessee, in 1862. The dog was paroled with the rest of the unit after six months. Jack, a brown and white bull terrier with the 102nd Pennsylvania, was captured twice by the Confederates in Virginia. The

Union officers of General Andrew Porter's staff in camp near the Chickahominy River in 1862. Second Lieutenant George Armstrong Custer is lying on the right, petting a dog that is camped with the men.

second time he was returned to his owners after being exchanged for a Confederate soldier.

Unusual animals

While many regiments were content to have a dog as a mascot, others chose less common animals. Some units seemed to enjoy the notoriety a mascot gave them within the army. The 43rd Mississippi, for example, picked up a camel somewhere on their travels and named it Old Douglas. The 43rd became known to other Confederates as the "Camel Regiment." Despite the fact that Old Douglas terrified horses and was almost uncontrollable, it stayed with the Mississippi soldiers until it

was killed by a Union sharpshooter at the Siege of Vicksburg in 1863.

On the Union side the 9th Connecticut Infantry kept a trained pig, which they called Jeff Davis as an insult to the Confederate president. The 2nd Rhode Island went to war with a sheep named Dick, until hunger got the better of the men and it was eaten, while the 12th Wisconsin Infantry kept a tame bear. Wisconsin regiments routinely adopted unusual mascots. There was the tame racoon of the 12th Wisconsin, the badger kept by the 23rd Wisconsin, and probably the most famous Civil War mascot of all, the bald eagle with which the 8th Wisconsin went to war (see box).

See also

• Camp life
• Monuments and
  souvenirs
• Morale
• Soldier life

OLD ABE

An eagle was presented to the 8th Wisconsin Regiment when it first mustered in Wisconsin and accompanied the regiment into 42 battles and engagements through Tennessee and Georgia. The eagle became known as Old Abe for President Abraham Lincoln. In action Old Abe was tethered to a large wooden perch decorated with a painted Union shield, carried by a soldier known as the eagle bearer. On occasions Old Abe would be set loose to fly above the fighting, and he became so well known that Confederates began calling him "the Yankee Buzzard." Despite Confederate efforts to kill or capture him, the bird stayed with the 8th Wisconsin until September 1864, when he was retired from active service. He was presented to the state of Wisconsin and housed in the state capital.

Union men of the 8th Wisconsin Regiment with their mascot, Old Abe. The eagle was often allowed to fly above the fighting.

Mason–Dixon Line

The original Mason–Dixon Line of the 1760s was the border dividing Maryland from Pennsylvania and Delaware. Later it was extended west and seen as the boundary between the Southern slave states and the free states of the North.

In 1760 Pennsylvania (which included present-day Delaware) and Maryland were both English colonies and were in dispute over their common border. A court in London decreed that the border would run north–south between Maryland and Delaware, and then west from Delaware along latitude 39° 43' North. Two Englishmen, a surveyor named Charles Mason and an astronomer, Jeremiah Dixon, were given the job of marking its position.

Their survey mission lasted from 1763 to 1767. As Mason mapped the route, Dixon found their precise latitude by means of the stars. In this way the pair charted the north–south line between Delaware and Maryland and then a line running 244 miles (393km) west from the Delaware border. The new boundary was marked every mile with blocks of limestone 5 feet (1.5m) long. In 1779 the line was extended farther to mark the border between Pennsylvania and what is today West Virginia.

Dividing the states

In the independent United States of the early 19th century the Mason–Dixon Line took on special significance in the debate over whether slavery should be permitted in the territories of the Louisiana Purchase. In 1820 the Missouri Compromise established a boundary between the Southern slave states and the free North, running west from the Mason–Dixon Line, south along the Ohio River, and then west along latitude 36° 30'. This new boundary was to become the broad frontline of the Civil War.

Charles Mason and Jeremiah Dixon laying out the boundary line separating Maryland and Pennsylvania in the 1760s. After mapping the route, they cut a broad path through the wilderness and marked the boundary line with blocks of limestone, many of which can still be seen today.

The original Mason–Dixon Line separated Pennsylvania and Delaware from Maryland and what is now West Virginia.

See also

- Causes of the conflict
- Kansas–Nebraska Act
- Missouri Compromise

Massachusetts

Massachusetts was one of the most steadfast supporters of the Union cause during the Civil War. Together with New York State, it was also a major center of the abolition movement to end slavery in the United States.

During the early years of Massachusetts history its colonists owned slaves, but by 1783 the practice had been abolished by the state legislature. In 1790 all slaves in Boston were freed, and in 1807 a Boston court heard the first law suit in the country aimed at integrating black children into white schools. The state's progressive attitudes to race continued. In 1843

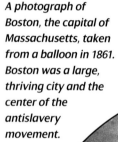

A photograph of Boston, the capital of Massachusetts, taken from a balloon in 1861. Boston was a large, thriving city and the center of the antislavery movement.

Massachusetts legalized interracial marriage, and in 1860 two free blacks were named as jurors to hear a trial in court. This was a radical move since African Americans did not then have legal rights as U.S. citizens.

Abolitionist movement

With this history of supporting and promoting civil rights, Massachusetts became a center for the abolitionist movement. By the 1850s attitudes within the movement were becoming more extreme in response to the increasingly aggressive demands from the Southern states for the legal protection of slavery and their right to maintain it. Many abolitionists, particularly in Massachusetts, became convinced that slavery could only be overthrown by violence. Such activists supported John Brown in his violent antislavery campaign in Kansas in 1855–1856. With their financial aid he moved into western Virginia in 1859 to launch the ill-fated attack on Harpers Ferry in October.

As the Southern states began to secede in late 1860, Massachusetts was one of the first states to respond in support of the Union. On January 18, 1861, Massachusetts offered President Lincoln men and money to uphold the authority of the United States, and this was followed on January 23 by a vote in the state legislature offering full support

MASSACHUSETTS BLACK REGIMENTS

Massachusetts was responsible for raising three black regiments: the 55th Infantry, the 5th Cavalry, and most famously the 54th Infantry, one of the first black regiments in the Union army. The state governor, John A. Andrew, a fervent abolitionist, saw the mustering of these regiments as an important step to winning the right of citizenship for blacks, and free men and former slaves alike responded to his call with enthusiasm. They traveled to Boston from throughout the North to enlist. The 54th Infantry was commanded by Robert Gould Shaw, from a prominent Boston abolitionist family. Among the regiment's recruits were Charles and Lewis N. Douglass, sons of the leading abolitionist Frederick Douglass. Andrew's faith in the courage of the

men to fight for their rights was more than justified on July 18, 1863, when the 54th took part in a charge on the Confederate-held Fort Wagner at Morris Island, Charleston. The heroic charge, although unsuccessful, spread the fame of the regiment and encouraged the recruitment of many more African Americans across the North.

The 55th Massachusetts Infantry marching through Charleston in February 1865.

for the continued existence of the Union. When war finally broke out in April 1861 and Lincoln appealed for volunteers, the state's reaction was immediate.

Massachusetts regiments

A number of regiments were quickly mustered into service. On April 18, 1861, just four days after Fort Sumter was bombarded by the Confederates, the 6th Massachusetts Infantry marched into New York past cheering crowds on its way to defend Washington, D.C. This regiment was among the first Union army units to suffer casualties. The 6th Massachusetts Infantry became the target of a large pro-Confederate mob as it marched through Baltimore, Maryland, on April 19 on its way to Washington. Four soldiers lost their

lives, and at least 40 more were injured in the riot. The 8th Massachusetts Infantry was then dispatched to Annapolis, Maryland, to keep the area under Union control. Three months later the 1st and 5th Infantry regiments were organized into the first Union army to take the field in Virginia and on July 21 were among the troops who fought the opening battle of the war at Bull Run, near Manassas. These units were among 77 infantry regiments mustered in Massachusetts during the war. In all, out of a total population of 1,231,000, Massachusetts supplied more than 152,000 men to fight for the Union cause.

See also

- Abolition
- Baltimore Riot
- Black troops
- Brown, John
- Bull Run (Manassas), First Battle of
- Shaw, Robert Gould

Meade, George G.

General George Gordon Meade (1815–1872) led the Union Army of the Potomac to victory at the Battle of Gettysburg in July 1863. A brave and conscientious leader, Meade had an explosive temper that could make his men wary of him.

Major General George G. Meade, the victor of Gettysburg. Despite his success in the battle, Meade was then sidelined by the appointment of General Ulysses S. Grant as general-in-chief of all the Union forces.

See also

- Bull Run (Manassas), Second Battle of
- Engineering, Military
- Gettysburg, Battle of
- Peninsular Campaign
- Potomac, Army of the

Meade was born in Cadiz, Spain, where his father was an American naval agent. After the family's return to their native land George Meade entered the U.S. Military Academy at West Point, graduating in 1835. After working as a civil engineer, he rejoined the U.S. Army in 1842 and fought in the Mexican War (1846–1848). He was then put in charge of a survey of the Great Lakes.

When the Civil War broke out, Meade was appointed brigadier general of volunteers and given command of a Pennsylvania brigade. He participated in General George B. McClellan's Peninsular Campaign in spring 1862 and the Seven Days' Battles at the end of June, where he was seriously wounded. He was not fully recovered when he returned to command his brigade at the Second Battle of Bull Run (August 1862). In recognition of his service there, and at Antietam a month later, Meade was promoted to major general of volunteers. In that capacity he commanded a division in the disastrous Union defeat at Fredericksburg (December 1862) and V Corps in a further Union defeat at Chancellorsville (May 1863).

Gettysburg

Despite the defeats, Meade's combat record was good. President Lincoln appointed him commander of the Army of the Potomac in June 1863, replacing General Joseph Hooker. Meade found himself up against Confederate General Robert E. Lee's Army of Northern Virginia, which had invaded Pennsylvania with the intention of delivering a knockout blow to the Union. At the Battle of Gettysburg (July 1–3) Meade showed great tactical skill, and after a titanic struggle Lee withdrew, his army shattered. Meade was criticized for not pursuing Lee's army after the victory. Nevertheless, the following January Meade received a congressional message of thanks for his success at Gettysburg.

Meade remained in command of the Army of the Potomac for the rest of the war. But when General Ulysses S. Grant was made general-in-chief of all Union forces in March 1864, Meade found himself effectively demoted and subject to Grant's orders. In August 1864 Meade was promoted to major general in the regular army and after the war remained in charge of various military departments until his death from pneumonia in 1872.

Medals and honors

At the beginning of the war neither the Union nor the Confederacy had a system of military decorations for valor. This remained the case in the Confederacy, but in 1861 the Union authorized the Medal of Honor for gallantry in action.

Winfield Scott, the general-in-chief of the U.S. Army at the beginning of the war, believed that the practice of awarding military decorations ran counter to the democratic nature of American society and its armed forces.

At the start of the war enlisted men on both sides could be recognized for bravery in several ways. They might be "mentioned in dispatches" to headquarters by their commanding officers or commended in person. Many Civil War commanders also made it a practice to mention by name in their battle reports soldiers who had performed with conspicuous bravery. The Confederate Congress published a "Roll of Honor" listing men cited for bravery after each battle and could also issue "Thanks of the Confederate Congress" to individual soldiers.

Awarding brevets

Officers enjoyed greater recognition for their exploits. They, too, were often mentioned in dispatches or in battle reports. Officers were also eligible for brevet promotions. Brevet ranks were honorary ranks higher than an individual's permanent rank, but carried no additional pay or authority. Thus an officer could hold two ranks, his official rank and a temporary brevet rank earned for gallantry. The Union army conferred brevet ranks quite frequently. The Confederate army had provisions to make brevet promotions, but did not award a single brevet.

Medal of Honor

Union President Abraham Lincoln signed into law in December 1861 the nation's first medal for gallantry in action, a "medal of honor" intended for U.S. Navy and Marine Corps enlisted men. The federal government extended this award to army enlisted men in July 1862 and then to army officers in March 1863.

The Union army awarded a total of 1,195 Medals of Honor during the war to 1,194 individual officers and men (Lieutenant Tom Custer, brother of General George Custer, earned two medals for separate acts). The first army Medals of Honor were presented by Secretary of War Edwin M. Stanton on March 25, 1863, to six men who

The Medal of Honor was created in 1861 and intended only to last for the duration of the war. In 1863 Congress voted to make it permanent. The Medal of Honor remains the highest award for valor in the United States.

THE MEDAL PURGE OF 1917

The Union Medal of Honor, although originally intended to honor acts of extraordinary bravery, was also awarded for many routine battlefield actions. Union recruiting officers frequently used them as rewards to encourage enlistment. This widespread distortion of the original intent of the Medal of Honor led the U.S. Army to revoke 911 medals in 1917. That included 864 presented to the members of one regiment, the 27th Maine Infantry, for standing ready to defend Washington, D.C., against a possible Confederate attack in July 1863. The commission also revoked the only medal ever awarded to a woman, Dr. Mary Edwards Walker, who assisted Union army surgeons during the war. Walker continued to wear her medal, however, and President Jimmy Carter formally reinstated it in 1977. Although several Union states minted and issued medals for gallantry, the Congressional Medal of Honor, along with brevet ranks and rolls of honor, remained the primary Union recognition of bravery in battle. The Medal of Honor continues in use to this day, while the last brevet rank was awarded in 1918.

Sergeant William H. Carney was the first African American to earn the Medal of Honor for his part in the Union attack on Fort Wagner in 1863. This picture dates from 1900, the year the medal was awarded.

had taken part in a daring attempt to steal an engine called *The General* in April 1862—an episode known as the "Great Locomotive Chase."

Some medals were backdated even further to honor acts of bravery near the beginning of the war. Francis Brownell was deemed by the Union to have committed the first act of bravery worthy of the Medal of Honor when he took part in an attempt to remove a Confederate flag from a tavern in Alexandria, Virginia, in May 1861.

Sergeant William H. Carney of the 54th Massachusetts Infantry was the first African American to earn a Medal of Honor when he helped lead his regiment's ill-fated assault on Fort Wagner, South Carolina, on July 18, 1863. A total of 16 African American enlisted men won the Medal of Honor during the war, adding luster to their already commendable combat record.

Confederate medals

The Confederate government did not introduce a system of military decorations and awarded only one medal for bravery. It was issued to the 49 members of an artillery battery known as the Davis Guard when they prevented a Union landing at Sabine Pass in Texas on September 8, 1863. The Davis Guard Medal had a green ribbon in honor of the battery's Irish heritage. After the war Confederate organizations raised funds to issue medals to veterans. In 1900 the United Daughters of the Confederacy issued the Southern Cross of Honor to Confederate veterans—giving out 12,500 crosses in one year. In 1977 the Sons of Confederate Veterans issued a Confederate Medal of Honor, which was awarded posthumously for bravery.

Medicine

With its huge armies and deadly weapons, the Civil War has often been described as the first modern war. Unfortunately for the participants, however, medical care and surgical treatment remained for the most part primitive.

In the 1860s doctors knew little more about the causes of infection and disease than they had known hundreds of years earlier. The existence of bacteria and viruses was still undiscovered. Surgeons operated with dirty instruments in filthy conditions, so even when injured soldiers had bullets removed or wounds sewed up, they were likely to face deadly infections. Combat wounds were not the greatest killers of Civil War soldiers, however. Disease took far more lives, and it created a huge problem that neither side in the war was able to solve.

When the war began in 1861, the United States army had only 113 surgeons in its ranks, 24 of whom resigned to support the Confederacy. Some doctors had attended medical schools, but many others had simply studied with other doctors and lacked the most basic knowledge of treating illness or injury.

A veteran leader

For the Union, medical matters fell under the authority of the Army Medical Bureau, which was led by an 80-year-old veteran of the War of 1812, Surgeon General Thomas Lawson. When he died in May 1861, he was replaced by Clement A. Finley, who did little to improve the bureau. Finley held the surgeon general's job until April 1862, when 33-year-old William A.

Hammond took his place. Hammond would bring much better leadership to the Medical Bureau, expanding its size and improving its professionalism.

The Union army did at least start the war with an existing medical service; the Confederates had to build theirs from nothing. The Confederate Medical Department was established by Samuel Preston Moore, who recruited doctors and nurses, set up procedures for treating the sick and wounded, founded hospitals, and eventually gave the Confederacy a medical service similar to that of the Union. Moore's task, though, was

A surgeon amputating a limb in an army field hospital in 1863. Amputations were carried out without antiseptics and often without anesthesia, and many patients died from either shock or infection.

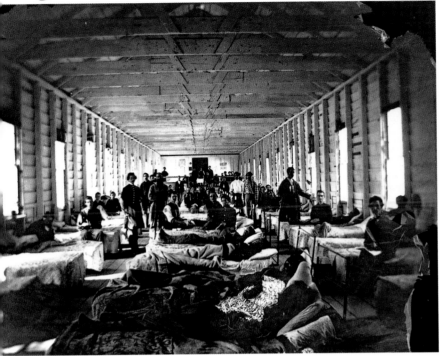

Soldiers wounded in the Civil War recovering in a hospital. The cramped conditions and lack of basic hygiene meant that many hospitals were breeding grounds for diseases that were as much a threat to life as the patient's original wounds.

that 25 percent of the soldiers were unfit for military duty.

The greatest threat to a soldier's life was disease. Historians estimate that diseases killed at least twice as many Civil War soldiers as combat wounds. That would mean that of the 620,000 soldiers who died in the Civil War, around 207,000 died from wounds and 413,000 from disease.

Disease did more than just reduce the number of men available to fight; it had a direct effect on many military campaigns. The Union's first attempt to take the city of Vicksburg in Mississippi in 1862 failed largely because more than half the troops were sick. Disease also figured in Lincoln's decision to abandon the Peninsular Campaign in Virginia that same year.

hampered by shortages caused by the Union naval blockade. Given the circumstances, Moore performed admirably in creating an effective medical department.

Unhealthy troops

Civil War commanders would have faced a tough job even if they had started the war with healthy troops. But many of the men who joined both armies were physically unfit. Early in the war men eager for military glory often tried to hide any illnesses or disabilities that might disqualify them from military service. As the war went on, and both sides became desperate for manpower, recruiting officers would overlook all but the most obvious physical handicaps. However, commanders soon learned that physically unfit troops were not merely useless in combat; caring for them took away valuable manpower and resources from the military effort. In 1862 an investigation in the Union army found

Fatal treatments

The treatments for disease were often as bad as the diseases themselves. The most common treatment for many diseases was calomel, a medicine whose main ingredient was mercury. Calomel depleted the body's vital fluids—already a major problem in diarrhea—and in large doses it could cause mercury poisoning. Some doctors still believed in the ancient practice of bleeding sick patients, which served only to weaken them further. Not surprisingly, many soldiers tried to avoid seeing a doctor unless they were on the verge of death. One of the few effective drugs available in the Civil War was quinine, which could prevent and treat malaria.

For those healthy enough to go into combat, a wound often meant death or the loss of a limb. Civil War muskets fired a very large lead bullet that traveled at a relatively slow speed, so bullets caused terrible wounds. Soldiers

KILLER DISEASES

The greatest killer of the war was probably dysentery (severe diarrhea). Nobody knew that dysentery was caused by bacteria, although some doctors suspected that there was a relationship between the cleanliness of army camps and the disease. Most soldiers gave little thought to using a nearby river as both a latrine and a drinking-water source. Simply boiling water before drinking it would have killed off the bacteria and saved countless lives, but nobody knew that. However, even when army doctors and officers instructed their men where best to place latrines, the men often disregarded their instructions.

Rivaling dysentery in deadliness were the diseases typhoid and pneumonia, which were even harder to prevent. A fourth major cause of death was the mosquito-born disease malaria, which was particularly severe in the South in the summertime.

Some diseases, like measles, mumps, and chicken pox, might not kill very many men but could cause such widespread sickness that they could make a company, a regiment, or an entire army unfit for duty. Sexually transmitted diseases such as gonorrhea and syphilis were another widespread problem.

---

with a head or gut wound were often left for dead. For arm and leg wounds amputation was the usual treatment to prevent death from gangrene infection. Some wounded solders were lucky enough to be treated by a surgeon supplied with chloroform or ether, anesthetics that made operations more bearable. Those less lucky—especially in the poorly supplied Confederate armies—could expect only whiskey and a bullet to bite on for the pain. Opium was also widely used as a painkiller.

Sanitary Commission

The Union's medical efforts were greatly assisted by a civilian volunteer agency known as the U.S. Sanitary Commission. Founded in June 1861, the commission was intended to conduct investigations and give advice on medical matters. Soon, however, its thousands of volunteers were raising money to buy bandages, medicine, and other necessities. Its inspectors tried to educate soldiers to keep their camps

A field surgeon's equipment included a box of surgical instruments and a very limited range of medicines. Although quinine was used successfully to treat malaria, a medicine such as calomel could kill as often as it cured.

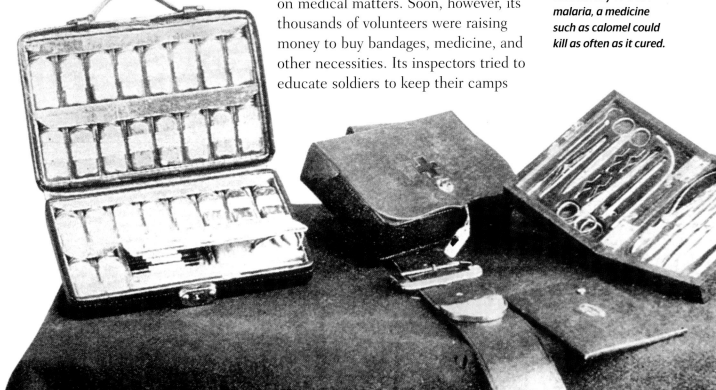

AMPUTATION AT A FIELD INFIRMARY

From Bell Irvin Wile's book *The Life of Johnny Reb*:

"I then went back to the field infirmary where I saw large numbers of wounded lying on the ground as thick as a drove of hogs in a log ... those shot in the bowels were crying for water. Jake Fellers had his arm amputated without chloroform. I held the artery and Dr. Huot cut if off by candle light. We continued to operate until late at night ... I was very tired and slept on the ground."

clean and therefore healthy. It also trained thousands of nurses and pushed the government to build more hospitals. The commission worked closely with a new unit of the Union army, the Ambulance Corps, which treated and evacuated wounded soldiers from the front lines. Many of the commission's practices were adopted by the Confederate Medical Department.

Women nurses

Work as nurses gave women their most direct role in the Civil War. At the beginning of the war nursing was still done by men, and there was much

resistance to having women exposed to the blood and suffering of hospitals. But these prejudices were gradually overcome as women proved their worth. By the end of the war some 3,200 women had served as nurses in the Union army. The Confederacy was slower to use female nurses, but it, too, finally put them to use, although in smaller numbers than the Union. The Confederacy also used slave women as nurses. Many civilian women who lived near major battlefields such as Gettysburg opened their homes to wounded soldiers and served as unofficial nurses. Some, like Clara Barton, who later founded the American Red Cross, simply worked as nurses on their own.

The war's main contributions to medicine were to train a new generation of surgeons and to open up the nursing profession to women. It also led to the creation of an ambulance corps. However, it was not until the 20th century that scientists began to understand the causes of many diseases and infections, and develop effective treatments for them.

Wounded soldiers recuperating under the trees on Marye's Heights, Virginia, in 1863. Marye's Heights was the scene of two fierce battles, the first of which took place during the Battle of Fredericksburg in 1862.

Memorials and souvenirs

Many Civil War soldiers took souvenirs from the battlefield to mark their experiences, while later generations have remembered the war with memorial ceremonies and by dedicating monuments to honor the dead.

Soldiers began creating memorials even before the war ended. Union officers built a monument on the battlefield at Manassas, Virginia, in 1864, making it the first Civil War battle site to be marked in this way. In the South before the end of the war organized women's groups began decorating the graves of the Confederate dead with flowers. This practice developed into an official Memorial Day, which was first observed in 1868 at the end of May, when the spring flowers were in bloom.

After many battles soldiers remaining near the site picked up souvenirs of their experiences such as bullets or buttons. Local citizens were also drawn to battlefields. On July 5, 1863, two days after the Battle of Gettysburg, a small boy was killed while souvenir-hunting. His older brother picked up a gun, still loaded, and it discharged.

Healing wounds

For those who survived the war memorials were a symbol of all they sacrificed in four arduous years. From 1865 to 1885 Southerners placed most of their monuments in cemeteries, evoking the grief and destruction caused by the war. After 1885 both Northerners and Southerners, working in veterans' groups or with state-level monuments committees, tended to place memorials on the battlefields

themselves. Gettysburg, Pennsylvania, the site of the war's largest battle and a turning point in the war, served as a natural focus of remembrance, especially by victorious Union veterans. The fields and woods of Gettysburg are filled with monuments of all styles,

The monument to the 132nd Pennsylvania at Antietam. It was dedicated on September 17, 1904, on the 42nd anniversary of the Battle of Antietam.

47

SOUVENIRS OF THE SURRENDER

On April 9, 1865, Union General Ulysses S. Grant and Confederate General Robert E. Lee met in the parlor of Wilmer McLean's house in Appomattox, Virginia, to agree to the terms for the surrender of Lee's army. The occasion transformed McLean's parlor into a historic location. When the meeting was over, Union officers who were present carried away every item in the room. General Philip Sheridan secured the small oval desk on which Grant wrote out the surrender terms and later presented it to General George A. Custer. Other officers cleaned out everything else, paying McLean for some items and simply stealing others. When everything else was gone, a staff officer made off with the room's carpet and a rag doll belonging to McLean's daughter. The doll remained in the officer's family for years after the war. Other observers who were not present at the conference dismantled the porch railings of the McLean house, and a Pennsylvania soldier carried off the seal of Appomattox County from the courthouse.

The McLean house, fitted with replica furniture to resemble the scene of Lee's surrender to the Union on April 9, 1865. Union officers took most of the original furniture as souvenirs.

including simple obelisks, grand amphitheaters, and realistic, intricate statues of fighting men.

Building monuments

The task of building Civil War monuments in the immediate postwar period was often divisive. Monument unveiling days in the South were events of enormous importance and became a focus of resistance to Republican policies. In Richmond, Virginia, on October 26, 1875, nearly 50,000 people attended the unveiling of General Thomas "Stonewall" Jackson's monument. The day included a parade and political speeches calling for the overthrow of Reconstruction.

Battlefield memorials

Beginning in the 1880s, the U.S. government initiated the process of turning the battlefields themselves into memorials by designating them national battlefields or national historical parks, with government staffing, funding, and protection from development. This takeover of the most prominent battlefields of the Civil War brought the process of remembrance under firm federal control.

In the 1870s Union general and former congressman Daniel Sickles, who lost a leg during the second day's fighting at Gettysburg, became the head of the New York State Monuments Commission. He played a key role in ensuring that the battlefield at Gettysburg was preserved as a memorial and even invested his own money in the project. He and others dictated the styles and placings of monuments at Gettysburg, and effectively prevented Confederate veterans' organizations from building monuments for a number of years. Even today, most Confederate memorials are confined to one area of the battlefield, around the start line of the second and third days' attacks.

When asked why he had not put up any monuments on the field to his noteworthy and controversial actions there, Sickles often replied, "The entire field is my monument." Perhaps the most bizarre of all Civil War memorials is Sickles' own leg, which was amputated at Gettysburg and remains on display at the Armed Forces Medical Museum in Washington, D.C.

Two capitals

Washington, D.C., and Richmond, Virginia, are filled with reminders of their Civil War past. Monuments and memorials dot the landscape of both cities, ensuring that residents and visitors alike never forget the war. In Washington more monuments exist to the Civil War than to any other single event; more equestrian statues stand there than in any other city in the United States. In addition, the Lincoln Memorial stands as a massive and fitting tribute to the wartime commander-in-chief. In it a statue of a seated Abraham Lincoln is surrounded by the texts of his wartime speeches and by a mural depicting the emancipation of the slaves.

In Richmond Hollywood Cemetery contains numerous graves and memorials to Confederate generals and thousands of Confederate soldiers. Monument Avenue, a broad thoroughfare on the edge of the downtown district, has a succession of late-19th-century memorials to the most famous Confederate generals from Virginia. They include the "Stonewall" Jackson monument and others to Robert E. Lee and J.E.B. Stuart.

Silent reminders

A memorial statue of a Civil War soldier stands in most small towns, especially those in the South. These monuments commemorate the local men who went to war. A monument at the University of North Carolina, affectionately known as "Silent Sam," remembers the students who fought. Such silent reminders ensure that Americans will never forget the cost of their Civil War.

A monument to the Confederate dead at Hollywood Cemetery in Richmond, Virginia. The 90-ft (27-m) high pyramid was built in 1869. Many Confederate bodies were removed from the battlefields around Richmond and reinterred at Hollywood.

Mexican War

In the Mexican War (1846–1848) the United States won a substantial area of land from Mexico. The political wranglings over whether these new territories should allow slavery or not intensified the divisions that led to the Civil War.

Union General Ulysses S. Grant described the Mexican War as "one of the most unjust ever waged by a stronger against a weaker nation." He argued that the Civil War was its direct result. "Nations, like individuals, are punished for their transgressions," he wrote. "We got our punishment in the most sanguinary [bloody] and expensive war of modern times." Grant was one of many Civil War generals who were officers in the Mexican War; others included Robert E. Lee, Pierre G.T. Beauregard, "Stonewall" Jackson, Don Carlos Buell, George B. McClellan, and George G. Meade.

Although historians are more reserved than Grant concerning the morality of the U.S. war with Mexico, most agree that the conflict was provoked by the United States, and that a strong causal link exists between it and the Civil War. For 25 years politicians had succeeded in keeping the divisive issue of slavery out of the national political arena. The Mexican War had the unintended effect of reintroducing the issue in a way that ultimately could not be contained.

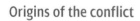

A portrait of Major General Winfield Scott and his ships landing at Veracruz, Mexico, in March 1847. Scott's campaign led to the capture of Mexico City in September, forcing Mexico to accept a negotiated peace.

Origins of the conflict

Texas was part of Mexico until 1836, when Anglo American settlers fought and won a war of independence. Texas became an independent republic and for nine years waged a sporadic border war with Mexico while hoping to be annexed by the United States. Mexico warned the United States that it would view the annexation of Texas as a hostile act. The U.S. government shied away from adding Texas to the Union until March 1845, by which time expansionist sentiment in the United States was strong.

Many Americans believed that the United States had a "manifest destiny" to dominate North America from coast

General Zachary Taylor (left) leads U.S. troops to victory against a larger Mexican force in the Battle of Buena Vista, fought near Monterrey, Mexico, on February 23, 1847.

to coast. President James Polk's administration agreed. It offered the Mexican government $15 million for present-day California and Arizona, New Mexico, Utah, and part of Colorado. The Polk administration also declared that the frontier between Texas and Mexico was the Rio Grande, not (as the Mexicans insisted) the Nueces River.

Course of the war

The Mexican government refused to sell what amounted to nearly half its territory. Nor did it budge on the question of the Nueces River boundary. The Polk administration sent an army under General Zachary Taylor to the mouth of the Rio Grande. Ulysses S. Grant explained: "We were sent to provoke a fight, but it was essential that Mexico commence it." Mexico obliged. In May 1846 Mexican forces crossed the Rio Grande and engaged Taylor's army in two sharp battles. The United States won both, Congress declared war, and the Mexican War had begun.

In the months that followed, U.S. forces easily grabbed the sparsely settled territory coveted by the United States. The Mexican government refused to accept the loss, however. The U.S. needed to achieve a victory decisive enough to force the Mexicans to the conference table. This was eventually accomplished in a remarkable campaign led by General Winfield Scott. In February 1847 Scott landed an army on the Mexican coast at Veracruz. His army slowly fought its way to the capital, Mexico City, which it captured on September 14. That forced the Mexican government to accept a negotiated peace.

The war formally ended in February 1848 with the Treaty of Guadaloupe Hidalgo, by which the United States got the land it wanted at a total cost of $18.25 million. About 80,000 U.S. troops fought in the war. Of them 1,750 were killed in action, and 11,550 died from disease. Scott later became the U.S. Army's top commander, a post he held at the start of the Civil War.

See also

- Grant, Ulysses S.
- Kansas–Nebraska Act
- Mexico
- Scott, Winfield

Mexico

Mexico was strategically important to both the North and the South. At the start of the Civil War Mexico was in turmoil. The U.S. preoccupation with the war left the way open for European powers to intervene in Mexico.

Don Matias Romero was Mexico's envoy in Washington during the Civil War. He had a good relationship with both Secretary of State William Seward and Union General Ulysses S. Grant.

See also

- Foreign relations, Confederate
- Foreign relations, Union
- France
- Mexican War
- Smuggling and piracy

In March 1861 Benito Juárez became president of Mexico following a three-year civil war that had ravaged the country. Both the Union and Confederacy wanted to establish good relations with the Juárez government. The Confederates wanted Juárez to allow their troops to travel through Mexico so they could invade California from the south. That would give them access to the state's gold and to ports on the Pacific Coast that were free of the Union blockade. However, Juárez was not prepared to allow Confederate troops into Mexican territory. The Confederate government tried and failed to stir up rebellion against Juárez in May 1861. It also attempted to negotiate directly with the governors of the virtually independent northern Mexican states, but with no success.

The Confederacy did manage to evade the Union blockade by exporting cotton through Matamoros, the Mexican town across the Rio Grande from Brownsville, Texas. Cotton was then transported 20 miles (32km) east, downstream to Bagdad on the Gulf of Mexico and from there to ports in the Caribbean and on to Europe.

The French emperor, Napoleon III, took advantage of the United States' preoccupation with the Civil War to extend French influence in the Americas. He used Mexico's failure to repay its foreign debts as an excuse to invade and installed Austrian Archduke Maximilian as a puppet monarch in 1864. Juárez fled north, from where he led a popular revolt against the French. President Abraham Lincoln adopted a position of neutrality on Mexico. Juárez declared: "It is enough for us that the North destroys slavery and does not recognize Maximilian." In fact, the Mexican envoy in Washington, Don Matias Romero, managed to persuade the U.S. government to look the other way while he arranged a shipment of arms to Juárez's forces in 1864.

Postwar U.S. pressure

With the end of the Civil War in 1865 the United States pressured the French to withdraw. The French occupation of Mexico ran contrary to the Monroe Doctrine of 1823, which declared that the United States would oppose further European colonization of the Americas. The French withdrew in 1867, leaving Maximilian to be defeated and executed in June. Juárez was reelected president in October.

Michigan

The outbreak of war found citizens of Michigan strongly opposed to secession. Most of the state's population had emigrated from New England and upstate New York since its creation in 1837, and it had strong economic ties to that area.

Settlers in Michigan retained their loyalty to the East and to the Union. The transportation highway of the Great Lakes and the Erie Canal further strengthened the links between Michigan and the East. The state's great railroad, the Michigan Central, connected the port city of Detroit with Chicago in 1852.

Michigan regiments

After the Confederate attack on Fort Sumter in April 1861 Michigan's Republican governor, Austin Blair, immediately called for a regiment of volunteers. When the state legislature met in May, it authorized the recruitment of 10 regiments. With patriotic fervor at a height many men could not find places in Michigan regiments. Hundreds of them enlisted in the service of other states; more than 50 out-of-state regiments counted Michigan men in their ranks. In all, about 90,000 Michigan men served in the Union army and navy—a remarkable record for a state whose entire population in 1860 numbered fewer than 750,000 people.

Michigan ultimately fielded 30 infantry regiments, along with 11 regiments of cavalry, a regiment of light artillery, one regiment of engineers, and another of sharpshooters. After the Union War Department authorized the recruitment of African American

soldiers in 1863, Michigan also furnished the 102nd U.S. Colored Infantry. About 14,700 Michigan soldiers lost their lives in the conflict.

24th Michigan Infantry

As in other Union states, Michigan's patriotism waned after the first year of war and the failure of the Union Peninsular Campaign. State authorities resorted to bounties to induce men to enlist after 1862. The state's most famous regiment, the 24th Michigan Infantry, was organized in Detroit after a mob broke up a recruiting rally in the city's center. To salvage Detroit's honor, residents organized the 24th Michigan—an extra regiment over and above the city's quota of men. The 24th Michigan joined the Army of the

Camp Blair in Jackson, Michigan. It was the state's main training camp and was named for the state's wartime governor, Austin Blair.

A view of Chicago from Michigan's main railroad, the Michigan Central, in 1863. The railroad linked Chicago with the state's port city of Detroit in 1852.

the Union as it was," but condemned the Emancipation Proclamation and Lincoln's suppression of civil rights. As Ethan Allen Brown, an Eau Claire farmer, declared in 1863, "I won't lick the dust off Old Abe's feet and say he can do no wrong." All the same, Lincoln, who had carried Michigan in the presidential election of 1860 by over 57 percent of the popular vote, won reelection in 1864 with nearly 56 percent of the state's votes.

Having fought from the First Battle of Bull Run (Manassas) through to Appomattox, Michigan soldiers were involved to the end. Troopers of the 4th Michigan Cavalry captured a disguised Jefferson Davis during his flight from Richmond, and members of the 24th Michigan Infantry served as the honor guard for Lincoln's casket on its funeral journey from Washington to Springfield.

Potomac's crack "Iron Brigade," served with distinction, and lost 399 of its 496 men at Gettysburg.

Opposition and dissent

Not all Michiganders, however, fully supported either the war or Lincoln. Many adamantly opposed a war against slavery. They volunteered or supported a war for "the Constitution as it is and

OUTSTANDING OFFICERS

The state contributed many outstanding officers to the Union cause. Israel B. Richardson, a Vermont-born West Pointer, had resigned from the army in 1855 and settled on a farm near Pontiac. He rose from the rank of colonel in the 2nd Michigan Infantry to major general of volunteers. Modest and, like Ulysses S. Grant, careless about his personal appearance (he once confessed that people called him "Greasy Dick"), Richardson won renown as a ferocious fighter. He was under consideration for command of the Army of the Potomac when he was mortally wounded at the Battle of Antietam (Sharpsburg).

Alpheus S. Williams was a Detroit lawyer who joined the Union army as a brigadier general in 1861. He commanded a corps at the battles of South Mountain, Antietam, and Gettysburg, and led the XX Corps on William T. Sherman's March to the Sea. Williams's lack of West Point credentials prevented his receiving the recognition he deserved. On the other hand, George A. Custer of Monroe earned fame as a cavalry commander by virtue of courage and self-promotion. Only 26 years old at the war's end, he personally accepted Confederate General Robert E. Lee's flag of surrender at Appomattox.

See also

• Antietam (Sharpsburg), Battle of
• Appomattox Campaign
• Bull Run (Manassas), First Battle of
• Davis, Jefferson
• Lincoln's assassination

Military academies, North and South

Military academies contributed much to the Civil War, especially the U.S. Military Academy at West Point, which trained more than 1,000 officers on both sides. On several occasions graduates found themselves fighting their former classmates.

In a young nation defended by citizen-soldiers, military academies became a fact of life in 19th-century America. President Thomas Jefferson set up the first national military school, the U.S. Military Academy at West Point, New York, in 1802. At first it was mainly an apprentice school for military engineers. In 1812, however, the academy was reorganized by an act of Congress. A new four-year course was introduced, and it became the main training facility for U.S. Army officers.

The Norwich system

Most Americans believed that military training contributed to a virtuous, disciplined, and law-abiding citizenry. As a result, a number of military schools were founded in the decades before the Civil War. Alden Partridge, a West Point graduate, founded a major Northern military academy in Norwich, Vermont, in 1819. The American Literary, Scientific, and Military Academy (now Norwich University) became a model for many other military academies. The academy combined instruction in arts and humanities with sciences and additional military training. Academy students wore uniforms, observed a military chain of command, and drilled with weapons. Military schools in Pennsylvania, New

York, New Jersey, and Massachusetts sprang up in imitation of the successful Norwich system.

Southern military academies

Several Southern military academies were set up as a result of the state militia system, under which the federal government required states to maintain arsenals of weapons and equipment for

Cadets from the U.S. Military Academy at West Point during the Civil War. Many of the leading generals in both the Union and Confederate armies were graduates of West Point .

Institute (VMI), established at the state arsenal in Lexington, the Citadel (the Military College of South Carolina) at the Charleston arsenal, and the Louisiana Military Academy, which had William T. Sherman, the future Union general, as its first president.

West Point graduates

The U.S. Military Academy at West Point contributed over 1,000 officers to the Civil War armies, in roughly equal proportion to each side. Of the 425 Confederate general-level officers, 146 were West Point graduates, compared to 217 of the 583 Union generals. Confederate President Jefferson Davis was also a West Point graduate.

Although many 19th-century military academies were shut down after the war, their legacy lives on in the state universities created under the Morrill Land Grant Act of 1862. The act gave federal assistance to states wishing to establish agricultural and mechanical colleges providing practical education, stipulating that these colleges must offer military instruction to students.

The Citadel, one of the military academies established at a state arsenal, can be seen in the middle distance of this view of Charleston, South Carolina, with the arsenal behind it.

See also

- Jackson, Thomas J.
- Sherman, William T.
- Virginia

use by militia units. State governments established military academies next to arsenals, thus providing guards for the equipment and providing weapons for use in military training. These schools caused little additional expense to the states and satisfied the demand for military readiness. They often offered scholarships for poor boys who would otherwise have been unable to attend. Examples include the most famous Southern school the Virginia Military

THE VIRGINIA MILITARY INSTITUTE

The Virginia Military Institute (VMI) was established at the state arsenal at Lexington, Virginia, in 1839. The school had the greatest impact on the Civil War of all of the country's military academies apart from the U.S. Military Academy at West Point. Its wartime superintendent, Francis H. Smith (a West Point graduate), supported the Confederate war effort by offering his cadets as drillmasters for newly formed volunteer regiments. The future Confederate General Thomas "Stonewall" Jackson, then a little-known instructor at VMI, led the cadets to Richmond in 1861 for this purpose. Although Jackson was

not himself a VMI graduate, he was to be forever associated with the school.

Two hundred VMI cadets fought at the Battle of New Market, Virginia, in May 1864—the only time a group of students fought as a unit in battle. They suffered 20 percent casualties. In total, VMI produced 20 generals, 90 colonels, and hundreds of junior officers for Confederate armies. In retaliation for the role of VMI cadets at New Market and the school's contribution to the Confederate cause, Union General David Hunter burned down the school in June 1864. VMI was rebuilt after the war.

Military Bands

Military bands were very important to the armies of the Civil War. Music not only raised the morale of the troops, but soldiers marched better and longer to a rousing tune. And bands provided entertainment in camp in the evenings.

The connection between music and soldiering was a close one. Not only were orders issued and passed from unit to unit by means of bugle and drum calls, but it was recognized that music put a spring in the step of a marching soldier and boosted his morale in battle. In fact, the military believed a rousing tune to be so essential to a soldier's fighting spirit that music bands were an official part of a regiment's organization.

Before the war U.S. Army regulations, which were later also adopted by the Confederacy, stated that an infantry regiment was allowed to enlist a band of 16 musicians, while each cavalry troop was permitted to enlist two musicians, which in an average cavalry regiment meant a mounted band of at least 20 men.

Aid to recruitment

Music also inspired volunteers to enlist. When the states of North and South issued their calls to arms in April 1861, they were made to the sound of patriotic tunes like "Bonnie Blue Flag" or "Yankee Doodle." Nothing encouraged young men to do their duty and join the ranks quicker than a rousing march, and enterprising recruiting officers made it a high priority to bring town or militia company bands into their new regiments to increase enlistment.

A fife-and-drum band of the Union army photographed in August 1863. Fife-and-drum bands were effective for marching and on the battlefield, and the fifes were not as heavy to carry as brass instruments.

In 1862 the Union army decided that regimental bands were a luxury it could no longer afford and discharged the musicians from service. However, brigades were still permitted to keep bands, and many musicians simply reenlisted to serve in them.

Musical instruments

Most military bands played brass instruments like tubas, horns, and bugles, accompanied by drums and other percussion instruments such as cymbals. Woodwind instruments like clarinets tended to be too fragile for army service, but fifes—a type of small flute—were very popular and widely used. Some regiments replaced their brass bands with corps of fifes and drums, instruments that were probably just as effective in stirring martial spirit, but cheaper to buy and easier to maintain and carry in the field than the brass ones.

The musical repertoire the bands played varied a great deal. Most bands were not restricted to playing marches but could turn their hands to dance music of the period such as polkas and waltzes as well as sentimental ballads and patriotic songs. That was important because their role in the regiments was not restricted to playing on the battlefield. Bands were essential as a source of entertainment to the soldiers in camp, and concerts were popular among the men and officers alike.

The quality of the music the bands produced also seems to have varied widely. The Confederates generally had the reputation of being musicians who played with more enthusiasm than skill or talent. One English visitor to a Confederate camp went so far as to describe the music he heard as "discordant banging."

However, the band of the Union 6th Wisconsin regiment had the reputation of being the worst military band of the whole war. The band could play only one song and was so poor at playing it that the regiment's commanding officer sent men to serve in the band as a punishment.

An African American military brass band, photographed in Washington in 1865. Brass instruments were the preferred instruments of most military bands during the Civil War.

Minnesota

At the outbreak of the Civil War in 1861 Minnesota was the first state to declare itself for the Union—despite the fact that it was a very new state, having been admitted to the Union in 1858, barely three years earlier.

On January 22, 1861, the Minnesota state legislators passed a resolution offering both men and money to preserve the Union. On April 13 Governor Alexander Ramsey was in Washington, D.C., when news came of the Confederate assault on Fort Sumter the previous day. He immediately offered Secretary of War Simon Cameron 1,000 Minnesota men for the Union cause. Ramsey's pledge was made two days before President Abraham Lincoln issued his Union-wide call for 75,000 troops.

Sioux uprising

Minnesota eventually provided the armed forces with 24,000 men. Although there were no Civil War battles in the state, there were serious clashes with resident Native Americans. As the state redirected more and more of its funds to the war effort, there was less food and money available for the inhabitants of the reservations. In the summer of 1862 an uprising by four disaffected Sioux led to the deaths of five white settlers. The Sioux feared a violent backlash and began arming for war. Over the next few days they killed more than 400 settlers. Many Minnesota troops had to be redeployed from the battlefields to put down the rising. After the Sioux were captured, 306 were sentenced to death, and 18 were sent to prison. However, thanks to the intervention of Lincoln, the death sentences of all but 39 of the prisoners were overturned.

Minnesota regiments

Meanwhile Minnesota regiments were involved in key engagements of the war. Most famously, on the second day of the Battle of Gettysburg in July 1863 the 1st Minnesota charged against overwhelming Confederate numbers, losing 215 of its 262 men. The 1st Minnesota had previously fought at First Bull Run on July 21, 1861, and suffered 180 casualties, more than any other Union regiment engaged. The 4th Minnesota also sustained heavy losses in Ulysses S. Grant's attack on Vicksburg on May 22, 1863.

See also

- Bull Run (Manassas), First Battle of
- Gettysburg, Battle of
- Home front, Union
- Vicksburg, Siege of

Minnesota troops engaged against rebellious Sioux in August 1862. Troops badly needed on the battlefields of the Civil War were diverted to fight the disaffected Sioux people.

Mississippi

Mississippi was the second state to secede from the Union. The state bore some of the heaviest losses in the Civil War—much of its land and property were devastated, and it is estimated that up to 60,000 of its inhabitants died.

The Civil War brought an end to a period of prosperity in Mississippi. The boom, which started in the early 1830s, was based mainly on the rapid rise in the world price of cotton, the state's main agricultural product. Mississippi also benefited from the sale of supplies to U.S. forces during the Mexican War (1846–1848).

Deepening division

As the controversy over slavery began to divide North and South in the 1850s, the white inhabitants of Mississippi resisted any suggestion of change. Their wealth and way of life were founded on slave-based agriculture. In 1860 there were 440,000 slaves in the state, 354,000 whites, and 800 free blacks.

After Abraham Lincoln's election as president in November 1860 South Carolina left the Union in December. Less than three weeks later, on January 9, 1861, the Mississippi legislature in the state capital, Jackson, passed the ordinance of secession and became the second state to join the Confederacy. The "Republic of Mississippi" was born, and there was rejoicing throughout the state. The women of Jackson presented the convention with the "Bonnie Blue Flag," which featured a single white star on a blue background and had come to symbolize Southern independence.

There was enormous enthusiasm for the war at first. In the early days so many Mississippians tried to enlist in the Confederate army that demand

Confederate troops, having burned what they could, evacuate the rail center of Corinth, Mississippi, in May 1862. The Union's capture of Corinth cut the Confederacy's east–west railroad link.

Confederate General John C. Pemberton's troops attack Union forces at the Battle of Champion's Hill, Mississippi, on May 16, 1863, in the last stages of the Union's campaign to capture the city of Vicksburg.

exceeded the commissions, equipment, and supplies available. About 80,000 Mississippians fought in the Civil War, and only 20,000 were accounted for at the war's end.

Military action

Many battles and engagements were fought in the state. Major military action began in spring 1862, and the Union captured the town of Corinth, a major railroad center, in May. Union gunboats had entered the mouth of the Mississippi River in April and captured New Orleans. The gunboats steamed upriver, taking Baton Rouge and Natchez, but were halted by the guns of the Confederacy's great stronghold at Vicksburg. It took almost a year for Union forces under Ulysses S. Grant to capture the vital river city. Several engagements in spring 1863 failed to stop the Union advance on Vicksburg. On May 14 Union troops entered the state capital, Jackson, partly burning the city and cutting the rail link to

Vicksburg. The Confederates retreated into the Vicksburg defenses. After a six-week siege the city fell to Union troops on July 4. Within days the capture of Port Hudson gave the Union control of the length of the Mississippi River.

Once the river was secured, Union armies advanced into the state. Most of the Confederate forces were transferred to other states after Vicksburg fell, leaving only cavalry units to protect the civilian population. This token defense was ineffective and caused great resentment among Mississippians, who felt that the Confederate government had abandoned them.

Union General William T. Sherman's troops marched from Vicksburg across the state to the rail center of Meridian in February 1864, destroying crops and railroad track as they went. Meanwhile, cavalry raiders from both sides were active across Mississippi, most notably Confederate cavalry commander Nathan Bedford Forrest. Few areas of the state escaped the ravages of war.

Mississippi River

The Mississippi in peacetime was a valuable trade link between North and South. In the Civil War it became a key strategic objective—both the Confederacy and the Union believed that whoever controlled the river would win the conflict.

The Mississippi is the second longest U.S. river, after the Missouri, and the largest—a third of all American streams empty into it. The Mississippi was used by Native Americans for trade and transportation for centuries before European colonization began. In the 17th century French settlers used it in the fur trade. By the 1800s the river was the principal outlet to the sea for the newly settled areas of the central United States. Goods were floated downstream to New Orleans and then shipped abroad. Imports were dragged upstream on rafts. The introduction of steamboats in 1811 meant that goods could be transported against the current much faster and led to a boom in river trade. This era was described in Mark Twain's *Life on the Mississippi* (1883).

Before engineers tamed the river in the decades after the Civil War, sailing on the Mississippi could be hazardous. The river was continually shifting its course, throwing up new sandbars and snags. The water level rose and fell at different times of the year. Submerged trees and other obstacles could tear a hole in the bottom of a boat.

Strategic objective

At the outbreak of the Civil War the Union general-in-chief Winfield Scott put forward a military strategy, dubbed the Anaconda Plan, that aimed to starve the Confederacy into submission by cutting it off from the outside world. Scott planned to send 60,000 men down from Illinois to seize control of the Mississippi. If the Union could gain control of the river, the Confederacy would be cut in half and would struggle to survive. The plan was never

The Union river gunboat USS **Fort Hindman** *patrolled the Mississippi RIver. It was a sidewheel steamer converted into a gunboat known as a "tinclad." It was lightly armored and with a shallow draft of 2–3 feet (0.6–1m).*

fully implemented, but control of the Mississippi remained an essential objective for the Union. It was important both politically and economically for President Abraham Lincoln for the North to have an outlet to the Gulf of Mexico to open up commerce for the states on the upper reaches of the Mississippi, where opposition to the war was strong.

The Confederacy needed to defend the vital transportation route and the rich agricultural lands of the lower Mississippi Valley. Although the South had fewer vessels than the North, it only needed to hold one strongpoint on the river to prevent any Northern commerce with the outside world. The Confederates fortified strategic points on the Mississippi with forts and gun emplacements and laid mines, then known as torpedoes, along the river.

Mississippi fleets

A wide variety of craft were used in the many battles on the Mississippi. Both sides had a number of rams—vessels whose chief weapon was an iron pole at the front—to hole and sink enemy ships. In 1861 the Union built ironclad gunboats at St. Louis known as "Pook Turtles" for their designer, James Pook, specifically to do battle on the lower Mississippi. The Union also used converted steamers, known as "tinclads" because their iron armor was only 1 inch (2.5cm) thick. This light armor was enough to protect against rifle fire from the river banks and allowed the tinclads to operate in shallower waters than heavily armored ironclads.

The Union combined navy and army forces to take the Mississippi. The navy transported troops and supplies, and bombarded forts, as well as fighting

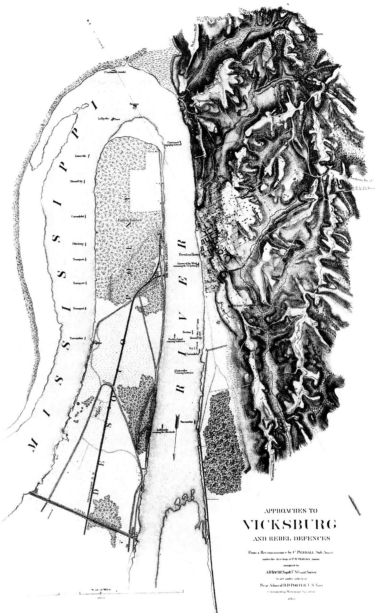

APPROACHES TO
VICKSBURG
AND REBEL DEFENCES

From a Reconnaissance by C. PRITALL. Sub Asst.
under the direction of F. H. Gerdes. Asst.
assigned to
A. D. BACHE, Supdt. U.S. Coast Survey
by act under orders of
Rear Admiral D. D. PORTER, U.S. Navy
Commanding Mississippi Squadron
1863

other vessels. For example, the fortified Island Number 10 near New Madrid, Missouri, was captured in April 1862 in a combined assault by troops and a fleet of gunboats and mortar boats.

The most important battles fought on the Mississippi were two great Union victories—the capture of New Orleans in April 1862 and of Vicksburg in July 1863 after a campaign lasting almost a year. Five days after Vicksburg fell, Port Hudson surrendered, and the length of the Mississippi was in Union hands.

An 1863 Union military map of Vicksburg and the surrounding Confederate defenses.

See also

- Anaconda Plan
- Farragut, David G.
- Ironclads
- New Orleans
- Vicksburg, Siege of
- West, the Civil War in the

Missouri

Missouri occupied a strategic position on the Mississippi and Missouri rivers and had abundant manpower and rich natural resources, so control of the state was very important for both sides in the Civil War.

An engraving of a painting by Missouri artist George Caleb Bingham, produced in 1872. It depicts Missouri settlers being ordered out of their homes by Union General Thomas Ewing (portrayed as the central figure) in retaliation for guerrilla raids in 1863.

Missouri became a state in March 1821 after a fierce debate in Congress over the expansion of slavery into the territories. Under the terms of the Missouri Compromise of 1820 Missouri entered the Union as a slave state, and Maine as a free state.

Most settlers moving into Missouri in the early 19th century came from slave states, so there was much sympathy for the South. However, there was also a large foreign-born population, many of whom supported the Union. In 1860 Missouri had a total free population (whites and free blacks) of nearly 1,070,000 and 115,000 slaves.

A convention was called in February 1861 to determine whether Missouri should secede, but delegates voted against the move. Hopes of maintaining neutrality in the state were dashed when Union troops under General Nathaniel Lyon invaded, pushing many former Union supporters into the Confederate camp. Claiborne Fox Jackson, Missouri's pro-Confederate governor, established the state guard and appealed for 50,000 volunteers to counter any invasion by Union troops. Like Kentucky, Missouri had two wartime state governments, one pro-Union and one pro-Confederate.

WILSON'S CREEK TO LEXINGTON

Of the 157 Civil War engagements fought in 1861, 66 were in Missouri. In August 1861 Brigadier General Nathaniel Lyon's Union Army of the West was involved in several skirmishes with Confederate forces, including Sterling Price's Missouri state guard. As the Missouri state guard and Confederate allies from Arkansas moved along Wilson's Creek toward Springfield on August 10, they clashed with Lyon's forces. The Battle of Wilson's Creek was the first major battle west of the Mississippi River. It was bloody, with more than 2,500 dead, injured, and missing—among them Nathaniel Lyon. The Confederate victory gave the South control of the Springfield area. Price built on his success by marching his troops north and capturing the Union garrison at Lexington. Encouraged by this success, in October 1861 Governor Claiborne Fox Jackson and other pro-Confederate legislators met in Neosho and passed an ordinance of secession. Confederate control of southwestern Missouri lasted until early 1862, when Union troops led by Samuel Curtis drove Confederate forces into Arkansas. The Union victory at Pea Ridge, Arkansas, in March 1862 kept organized Confederate forces out of Missouri until 1864.

The Battle of Wilson's Creek near Springfield on August 10, 1861, marked the start of the Civil War in Missouri.

During the war various armed forces ranged over the state, causing great suffering to the local population. Union troops moved back and forth to keep Southern troops out. The Confederates launched two major campaigns into Missouri, directed by the former state governor, Sterling Price, in 1861 (see box) and again in 1864. All the while, guerrilla bands allied to one or the other side were active. They murdered opponents, burned homes, looted businesses, and slaughtered livestock. Missouri saw more military action in the war than all other states apart from Tennessee, Virginia, and Georgia.

The Battle of Westport

Sterling Price led the Confederacy's second big attempt to break the Union hold on Missouri in September 1864. He marched from Princeton, Arkansas, with more than 8,000 troops bound for Missouri. By the end of October he and his troops had marched nearly 1,500 miles (2,400km) and fought 43 engagements, but the campaign failed. The final showdown was at Westport, Missouri, on October 23, when Price's Confederates were beaten by Samuel Curtis's 20,000-strong Union Army of the Border. There were about 1,500 casualties on each side. Westport, sometimes known as "the Gettysburg of the West," was the largest battle fought west of the Mississippi. The battle marked the end of organized Confederate resistance in Missouri, though guerrilla warfare continued.

See also

- Guerrilla warfare
- Immigrants
- Kansas–Nebraska Act
- Missouri Compromise
- West, the Civil War in the

Missouri Compromise

The Missouri Compromise of 1820 aimed to keep a balance of free and slave states and prevent conflict over the expansion of slavery from splitting the nation. It kept the peace between North and South for over 30 years.

Henry Clay was a skillful Kentucky politician who was largely responsible for getting the Missouri Compromise of 1820 accepted by Congress. Thirty years later, in 1850, Clay was instrumental in getting a further compromise measure passed.

Disagreements over slavery had existed since before the American Revolution. Southerners at the 1787 Constitutional Convention had demanded that each state be allowed to decide for itself whether or not it wanted slavery. Although this addressed the question of slavery in existing states, the Constitution was less clear about permitting slavery in newly created states. That became a major issue in 1819, when the territory of Missouri applied for statehood.

Congress had to pass a law to grant Missouri statehood. As the legislation was being debated in the House of Representatives in February 1819, Representative James Talmadge of New York proposed an amendment that would eventually free the slaves already in Missouri (in 1819 there were about 10,000 slaves in the state) and prevent any more from being taken there. This move provoked a bitter debate about slavery and whether the government had any right to restrict it. Some Northern congressmen wanted to stop the westward spread of slavery as a first step to abolishing it altogether. For Southerners it was a matter of equal rights—if Northerners could take their property into the west and settle there, Southerners should be allowed to bring their slave property. The question of Missouri was also important because at the time the number of free states and slave states was equal, and so the Senate was evenly balanced between free-state and slave-state senators. Any laws passed had to be supported by politicians from both sides. The addition of Missouri on either side would upset the balance.

Although the House of Representatives passed the Missouri bill, Southerners in the Senate blocked it. Congress adjourned with no action having been taken. When Congress met again in December 1819, the debate raged furiously, with Southerners declaring in Congress for the first time that slavery was a "positive good" for slaves, masters, and the nation. From Virginia the former President Thomas Jefferson wrote that the Missouri controversy, "like a firebell in the night, awakened and filled me with terror."

Details of the Compromise
As Jefferson understood, the Missouri crisis could have led to civil war in 1820. However, Speaker of the House Henry Clay championed a compromise that he hoped would satisfy both

Northerners and Southerners. Clay first proposed that a new state, Maine, be carved out of northern Massachusetts. Maine would become a free state, and Missouri would be allowed to enter as a slave state, keeping an even balance of power in the Senate. To avoid any future problems of this kind, Jesse B. Thomas, an Illinois senator, proposed that a line be drawn on the map across the country along the latitude of 36° 30' (the latitude of the southern border of Missouri). All states created north of the line would be free, and all states south of the line would be slave. In the future new states would enter the Union in pairs, one free and one slave, just as Missouri and Maine had. Clay used his charm and political ability and succeeded in getting the compromise passed, and Missouri was admitted to the Union in March 1821.

The Missouri Compromise originally only applied to the territory bought from France in the 1803 Louisiana Purchase, which extended from the present-day state of Louisiana in a northwesterly direction all the way to Oregon. Texas, California, and the rest of the Southwest still belonged to Spain. Over the following 30 years most Americans came to view the Missouri Compromise as a sacred agreement between the North and South that would forever prevent a civil war over slavery.

Recurring dispute

When the United States gained Texas in 1845 and the rest of the Southwest in 1848 after the Mexican War, the issue of slavery in the territories rose again. The Compromise of 1850 temporarily averted the dissolution of the Union, but the Kansas–Nebraska Act of 1854 repealed the Missouri Compromise, and the issue could no longer be compromised away. War came in 1861. Jefferson had been right when he predicted in 1820 that the Missouri Compromise was "a reprieve only, not a final sentence."

See also

- Abolition
- Dred Scott case
- Kansas–Nebraska Act
- Mexican War
- Slavery

A symbolic group portrait of 1852 celebrates the efforts in Congress to preserve the Union, especially the Compromise of 1850. Henry Clay, who was important in the compromise measures of 1820 and 1850, is seated third from left. By the late 1850s, however, compromise was no longer possible.

Mobile

Mobile, Alabama, the Confederacy's second largest Gulf port, escaped direct attack in the war. It was an important shipbuilding center, and some trade continued from the port until the Union captured Mobile Bay in August 1864.

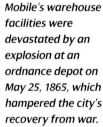

Mobile's warehouse facilities were devastated by an explosion at an ordnance depot on May 25, 1865, which hampered the city's recovery from war.

Mobile's location made it a target for Union blockaders. Initially the blockade was ineffective, as the Union only closed off the main entrances to Mobile Bay, leaving others unguarded. Trade continued between New Orleans, Mobile, and Havana by bayou and inland channels until New Orleans was captured in April 1862. Blockade-running decreased sharply after this and was halted by the capture of Mobile Bay in August 1864, when a Union fleet led by David G. Farragut braved sea mines to enter the bay and overwhelm Confederate ships.

Mobile was a railroad center from which supplies were shipped north to Confederate armies. The city also handled much east–west rail traffic because of gaps in the Confederacy's rail system. Many ships were built in Mobile, and ironclads, such as the CSS *Tennessee*, were armed there. The first successful submarine, the CSS *Hunley*, was built in Mobile in 1863.

Despite the blockade, Mobilians enjoyed a vibrant social life. Naval officers socialized in fashionable homes and feted their hosts with shipboard balls, dinners, and cruises. A newspaper dubbed Mobile the "Paris of the Confederacy." The population of the bustling port city grew from 30,000 in 1860 to about 45,000 by 1865.

Shortages and inflation

As in other blockaded cities, shortages and high inflation caused hardship. City authorities sponsored a market for poor citizens, and private organizations also provided relief. These efforts failed to avert a bread riot in 1863 by women protesting shortages and high prices.

The Confederate embargo and Union blockade substantially reduced the cotton trade through Mobile for the duration. Mobile survived the war physically intact, only to lose most of its warehouse facilities on May 25, 1865, in an ordnance depot explosion.

Mobile Bay, Battle of

After capturing New Orleans and gaining control of the Mississippi River, the Union targeted Mobile Bay. On the morning of August 5, 1864, Union naval forces under David G. Farragut sailed into the bay and began to attack.

The main entrance to Mobile Bay was defended by Fort Morgan with 40 guns and Fort Gaines with 16 guns, and there were sea mines (known as torpedoes) placed along the channel. Confederate forces under Franklin Buchanan consisted of the powerful ironclad CSS *Tennessee*, three wooden ships, 427 men, and 22 guns. David G. Farragut led a Union fleet of 14 wooden ships, four ironclad monitors, 2,700 men, and 197 guns.

"Go Ahead!"

The Union ironclad USS *Tecumseh* fired the first shot as the Union fleet entered the channel on August 5. Wooden ships were fastened together in pairs to face the heavy fire from Fort Morgan. The *Tecumseh* hit a mine and sank quickly. At its sinking the captain of the leading ship, the USS *Brooklyn*, halted in confusion and signaled for advice from Farragut. From his flagship, the USS *Hartford*, Farragut issued his famous rallying order: "Damn the torpedoes! Go ahead!"

The *Hartford* then led the rest of the Union fleet into the bay without losing another vessel. They soon overwhelmed the three wooden Confederate ships. For almost two hours the *Tennessee* continued the fight alone against the entire Union fleet. Its six-inch-thick iron armor was pounded with solid shot. At least three Union ships

repeatedly rammed the *Tennessee* at full speed. Surrounded by enemy ships, the badly damaged *Tennessee* surrendered. The three-hour battle ended in a Union victory. Each side lost 300 men killed, wounded, or captured. The city of Mobile remained in Confederate hands for eight months, but the Union had achieved its goal of closing the port.

By the third week in August Union troops had suceeded in capturing Fort Powell, which guarded Grant's Pass into Mobile Bay, and Forts Morgan and Gaines at the bay's main entrance. The Union victory at Mobile Bay, along with the capture of Atlanta, Georgia, on September 2, boosted Northern morale and Abraham Lincoln's chances of reelection as president in November.

Outnumbered by 17 to 1, the Confederate ironclad CSS Tennessee (center) continued the Battle of Mobile Bay alone after the other Confederate ships were overwhelmed. After nearly two hours the ironclad finally surrendered.

See also

- Alabama
- Confederate navy
- Farragut, David G.
- Ironclads
- Naval warfare
- Union navy

Glossary

blockade-runner
A sailor or ship that broke through the Union blockade of Southern ports during the Civil War. Ships used in blockade-running were often specially built. They were fast and difficult to spot.

brevet rank
A promotion for an army officer to a higher rank, often as a honor just before retirement. There was no increase in pay and a limited increase in responsibilities.

brigade
A military unit consisting of between two and six regiments. The brigade was the common tactical unit of the Civil War.

casualty
A soldier lost in battle through death, wounds, sickness, capture, or missing in action. The huge number of casualties suffered by both sides during the Civil War—an estimated 620,000—was unprecedented.

commerce raider
A Confederate ship that targeted Union merchant shipping to undermine the North's ability to trade.

company
A military unit consisting of 50 to 100 men commanded by a captain. There were 10 companies in a regiment. Companies were raised by individual states.

conscription
Compulsory enrollment of able-bodied people into the armed forces, usually during a national emergency. Although unpopular, conscription was used by both the Union and the Confederacy.

corps
The largest military unit in the Civil War armies, consisting of two or more divisions. Corps were established in the Union army in March 1862 and in the Confederate army in November 1862.

division
The second largest military unit in the Civil War armies. A division was made up of three or four brigades and was commanded by a brigadier or major general. There were between two and four divisions in a corps.

habeas corpus
A legal protection against being imprisoned without trial. President Abraham Lincoln was severely criticized for suspending the right to trial in the Union during the war. President Jefferson Davis took a similar unpopular measure in the Confederacy.

mine
Known during the Civil War as "torpedoes," mines are explosive devices, usually concealed, designed to destroy enemy soldiers and transportation. Although considered at the time to be outside the bounds of acceptable warfare, they were used extensively in the Civil War.

mortar
A type of short-barreled cannon that threw shells in a high arc over enemy fortifications. They were usually used in siege warfare.

parole
Captured prisoners at the beginning of the war were exchanged and paroled, which meant they gave their word that they would not fight any more. The system became increasingly unworkable. Union authorities restricted the practice when they realized it was the main means by which the Confederacy replenished its troops.

partisan raiders
Irregular bands of troops, authorized by the Confederate government in April 1862 to operate behind enemy lines. They wore uniforms and were paid for captured war material they gave to the government. Despite some notable

successes, their overall usefulness to the Southern war effort has been disputed.

regiment
A military unit consisting of 10 companies of 100 men at full strength. In practice, however, most Civil War regiments were much smaller than this. Raised by state governors, they were usually composed of men from the same area. The Civil War soldier's main loyalty and sense of identity was connected to his regiment.

rifling
A technique used on both guns and cannons that allowed weapons to fire further and with greater accuracy than previously. Rifled barrels had spiral grooves cut into the inside, which gave a bullet or shell spin when fired.

secessionist
A person who supported the breaking away of the Southern states from the United States and thus a supporter of the Confederacy.

skirmishers
Infantrymen trained to fight in open order rather than the closed ranks of ordinary soldiers. They were often used ahead of the main force to prepare the way for a main attack or as snipers to harass an enemy counterattack.

sutler
A camp follower who sold provisions to the soldiers to supplement their army rations. Sutlers usually had a semi-official status and were attached to specific regiments. They were often resented for charging very high prices.

volunteer
A civilian who fights when his country goes to war, often because of personal convictions, a sense of adventure, or for a bounty or enlistment fee. The majority of Civil War soldiers were volunteers, rather than regular soldiers.

Further reading

Alleman, Tillie Pierce. *At Gettysburg, or What a Girl Saw and Heard of the Battle: A True Narrative*. New York: W. Lake Borland, 1889.

Berlin, Ira, et al. (editors). *Free at Last: A Documentary History of Slavery, Freedom, and the Civil War*. New York: The New Press, 1992.

Billings, John D. *Hardtack and Coffee, or the Unwritten Story of Army Life*. Boston: George M. Smith, 1887.

Bradford, Ned (editor). *Battles and Leaders of the Civil War*. New York: Dutton, 1956.

Catton, Bruce. *The Civil War*. Boston, MA: Houghton Mifflin, 1987.

Clark, Champ, and the editors of Time-Life Books. *The Assassination: Death of the President*. Alexandria, VA: Time-Life Books, 1987.

Coggins, Jack. *Arms and Equipment of the Civil War*. New York: Doubleday, 1962.

Damon, Duane. *When This Cruel War Is Over: The Civil War on the Home Front*. Minneapolis, MN: Lerner Publishing, 1996.

Engle, Stephen D. *The American Civil War: The War in the West 1861–July 1863*. London: Fitzroy Dearborn, 2001.

Evans, Charles M. *War of the Aeronauts*. Mechanicsburg, PA: Stackpole Books, 2002.

Faust, Patricia L. (editor). *Historical Times Illustrated Encyclopedia of the Civil War*. New York: Harper and Row, 1986.

Gallagher, Gary W. (editor). *The Wilderness Campaign*. Chapel Hill, NC: University of North Carolina Press, 1997.

Gallagher, Gary W. *The American Civil War: The War in the East 1861–May 1863*. London: Fitzroy Dearborn, 2001.

Gallagher, Gary W., and Robert Krick. *The American Civil War: The War in the East 1863–1865*. London: Fitzroy Dearborn, 2001.

Glatthaar, Joseph T. *The American Civil War: The War in the West 1863–1865*. London: Fitzroy Dearborn, 2001.

Grant, Ulysses S. *Personal Memoirs*. New York: Crescent Books, 1995.

Hendrickson, Robert. *The Road to Appomattox*. New York: John Wiley, 1998.

Kelbaugh, Ross J. *Introduction to Civil War Photography*. Gettysburg, PA: Thomas Publications, 1991.

McPherson, James M. *Battle Cry of Freedom*. New York: Oxford University Press, 1988.

Marrin, Albert. *Commander in Chief: Abraham Lincoln in the Civil War*. New York: Dutton, 1997.

Oates, Stephen B. *A Woman of Valor: Clara Barton and the Civil War*. New York: Macmillan/Free Press, 1994.

Robertson, James I. *Soldiers Blue and Gray*. Columbia, SC: University of South Carolina Press, 1998.

Schindler, Stanley (editor). *Memoirs of Robert E. Lee*. New York: Crescent Books, 1994.

Smith, Gene. *Lee and Grant: A Dual Biography*. New York: McGraw-Hill, 1984.

Trudeau, Noah. *Like Men of War: Black Troops in the Civil War, 1862–1865*. New York: Little, Brown, and Co, 1998.

Van Woodward, C. (editor). *Mary Chesnut's Civil War*. New Haven, CN: Yale University Press, 1981.

Wiley, Bell Irvin. *The Life of Johnny Reb: The Common Soldier of the Confederacy*. Baton Rouge, LA: Louisiana State University Press, 1980.

Wiley, Bell Irvin. *The Life of Billy Yank: The Common Soldier of the Union*. Baton Rouge, LA: Louisiana State University Press, 1981.

Wright, Mark. *What They Didn't Teach You about the Civil War*. Novato, CA: Presidio Press, 1996.

Useful websites:

These general sites have comprehensive links to a large number of Civil War topics:
http://sunsite.utk.edu/civil-war/warweb.html
http://civilwarhome.com/
http://americancivilwar.com/
http://www.civil-war.net/

http://www2.cr.nps.gov/abpp/battles/bystate.htm
This part of the National Parks Service site allows you to search for battles by state

http://pdmusic.org/civilwar.html
Sound files and words to Civil War songs

http://www.civilwarmed.org/
National Museum of Civil War Medicine

http://memory.loc.gov/ammem/aaohtml/exhibit/aopart4.html
Civil War section of the African American Odyssey online exhibition at the Library of Congress

http://valley.vcdh.virginia.edu/
The Valley of the Shadow Project: details of Civil War life in two communities, one Northern and one Southern

http://etext.lib.virginia.edu/civilwar/CivilWarBooks.html
Texts from the Civil War period online, including letters, poetry, and speeches

http://www.civilwarhome.com/records.htm
Battle reports by commanding generals from the Official Records

http://www.cwc.lsu.edu/
The United States Civil War Center at Lousiana State University

http://www.nps.gov/gett/getteducation/bcast20/act05.htm
Civil War slang

http://home.ozconnect.net/tfoen/
Original articles and images of the Civil War navies

http://civilwarmini.com/
Quizzes and interesting facts about the Civil War

Set Index

Page numbers in **bold** refer to volume numbers. Those in *italics* refer to picture captions, or where pictures and text occur on the same page.

THE CIVIL WAR

PICTURE CREDITS
Front cover: **London Library-Battles and Leaders of the Civil War, 1888:** top left, top right; **Library of Congress:** top center, bottom right; Title page:**Library of Congress.**

Antietam National Battlefield/Jim Strogin: 47; **Corbis:** 27, 38, 55, 68; **Bettmann:** 7,14, 15, 16, 35, 37; **Lee Snider:** 48; **Getty Images:** 18, 24, 34; **Library of Congress:** 5, 6, 8, 9,12, 19, 20, 21, 22, 26, 28, 29, 30, 32, 33, 39, 42, 46, 49, 51, 54, 56, 57, 58, 59, 62, 64, 65, 66, 67, 69; **National Archives:** 10, 11, 13, 17, 23, 25, 40, 43, 44, 50, 52, 53, 60, 61, 63; **National Library of Medicine:** 45; **Robert Hunt Library:** 4; **State Historical Society of Wisconsin Visual Archives:** 36; www.lindapages.com: 41.